THE
365 BULLET
GUIDE

Organize your life creatively,
one day at a time

ZENNOR COMPTON

Designed and illustrated by
Marcia Mihotich

FLATIRON
BOOKS
NEW YORK

www.flatironbooks.com

The Library of Congress Cataloging-in-Publication Data is available upon request

ISBN 978-1-250-17185-6 (trade paperback)

Our books may be purchased in bulk for promotional, educational, or business use. Please contact your local bookseller or the Macmillan Corporate and Premium Sales Department at 1-800-221-7945, extension 5442, or by email at MacmillanSpecialMarkets@macmillan.com.

Originally published in the UK by Boxtree, an imprint of Pan Macmillan

First U.S. Edition: October 2017

10   9   8   7   6   5   4   3   2

CONTENTS

INTRODUCTION

The 365 Bullet Guide isn't a diary, nor is it a notebook. Rather, it's a launch pad for an infinitely customizable organization system that will change your life. These pages will help you to put all your planners, to-do lists and journals in one book. The only essential extras are a notebook (see page 9 for advice on what kind to choose) and a pen.

The joy of a bullet book is that it can be as simple or as complicated as you like. Whether you need to monitor multiple projects at work, want to keep tabs on your domestic chores, track your health, improve your mood or need a place to store personal goals and precious memories, or all of the above, a bullet book is an invaluable resource. Here there are enough bulleting steps, activities and ideas for every day of the year, most of which will take you 365 seconds or less. However insignificant such bursts of organizational creativity may seem, the greatest ideas start small.

Dotted throughout the book are Get Creative pages, which will inspire you to embellish your pages with colors, shapes, boxes, borders and doodles, and even teach you some lettering techniques.

There is plenty of space to practice within this book but you might want to have some scrap paper to hand, particularly if you're a perfectionist. There are tips on how to fix mistakes in the book, but don't beat yourself up if your pages don't look as perfect as you'd like. You'll find your own style.

So let's begin.

GET STARTED

CHOOSING YOUR JOURNAL

Select your bullet book carefully. It will undergo a lot of use so pick a sturdy one. You'll be drawing both horizontal and vertical lines so you might want to pick a notebook that has grids or dots on each page. If your to-do lists are very long, then pick a book with lots of pages. If you're more of a minimalist, then slim is fine. Numbered pages save time but they're not essential, you can do this yourself.

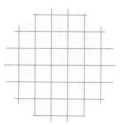

SET-UP

If your notebook is completely blank, number the pages or be sure to number them as you go along. You can number every other page if you're pushed for time.

On the first page, add a title (it can just be your name). Alternatively, leave this blank and come back once you've had some practice with lettering, borders and doodles.

On the next page, add your heading: INDEX. The Index will act as a contents page for your journal. It will allow you to keep track of the different spreads you add to your book by using their title and page number. As your journal gets longer, you'll be able to find what you're looking for at a quick glance. If your notebook is particularly thick, you may want to allocate two pages for the Index. You can leave it blank for now.

Set-up variations

If you want to keep your work and personal lives separate, then use opposite ends of the book. Consider creating an Index for each. For more set-up ideas, check out the Masterclass section at the back of the book.

Index

THE KEY

The main principle of bulleting can be summed up using a very simple key of symbols that will represent the different types of things that could appear on your to-do list. These symbols will be used throughout your journal so it will be useful to have this at the start of your book, allowing you to refer back to it when you need.

You can start bulleting your daily routine by using the following key for your to-do list:

☐   Tasks are represented by empty squares.

■   Completed tasks can then be filled in.

○   Events are represented by small circles.

—   Notes can be represented by a dash.

AT THE END OF THE DAY

Chances are you didn't manage to tick off everything on your list but the bullet method ensures that no task is ever left behind. Use chevrons to mark anything you need to carry over to tomorrow. This is known as migrating.

■ Set meeting with Sarah

○ Catherine's going away party

— Must try to drink more water today

☐ Laundry

- - - - - - - - - - - - - - -

☐ > Laundry

jan	feb	mar
M T W T F S S 1 2 3 4 5 6 7 8 9 10 11 12 13 14 15 16 17 18 19 20 21 22 23 24 25 26 27 28 29 30 31		
apr	may	jun
jul	aug	sept
oct	nov	dec

YEARLY

Now we're going to add a handy year-long calendar for reference. This is your Yearly. You might want to try this in pencil first, or measure your months with a ruler. This can be spread over a double page depending on how much space you want to allocate for each month. Alternatively, go to *panmacmillan.co.uk/365bulletguide* where you can download and print these at the size of your choice. Once you've finished, make a note of the page numbers to use in your newly created Index.

Variations

Block off holidays, exam season or other big events in your Yearly so that you can see your plans at a glance.

	march	april	may	june
1				
2				
3				
4				
5				
6				
7				
8				
9				
10				
11				
12				
13				
14				
15				
16				
17				
18				
19				
20				
21				
22				
23				
24				
25				
26				
27				
28				
29				
30				
31				

---

january						
M	T	W	T	F	S	S
				1	2	3
4	5	6	7	8	9	10
11	12	13	14	15	16	17
18	19	20	21	22	23	24
25	26	27	28	29	30	
31						

february

march

april

may

june

_____

April	May	June

April

M	T	W	T	F	S	S
			1	2	3
4	5	6	7	8	9	10
11	12	13	14	15	16	17
18	19	20	21	22	23	24
25	26	27	28	29	30

_____

_____

_____

_____

_____

_____

_____

_____

jan	feb	mar

apr	may	jun
	M T W T F S S	
	1 2 3	
	4 5 6 7 8 9 10	
	11 12 13 14 15 16 17	
	18 19 20 21 22 23 24	
	25 26 27 28 29 30	
	31	

_____

_____

_____

_____

FUTURE LOG

Add a Future Log like the one below. This is where you'll
keep track of those tasks and dates that you need to
remember in the future. It's essentially a brain dump that
will allow you to focus on the tasks at hand, rather than
worry about those upcoming. If you're a minimal note-taker
then you'll only need a double page for this. Otherwise,
space this over two double pages. Not sure? Don't worry,
you can start again further in the book. Make a note of key
dates like birthdays, holidays and anniversaries. Now, once
again, make a note of the page numbers to use in the Index.

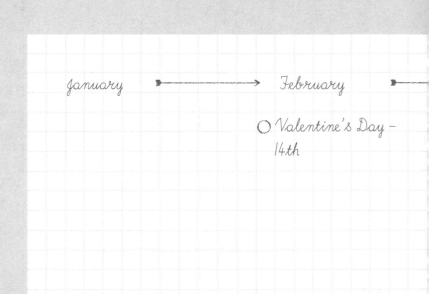

March $\longrightarrow$ April $\longrightarrow$

☐ Taxes due

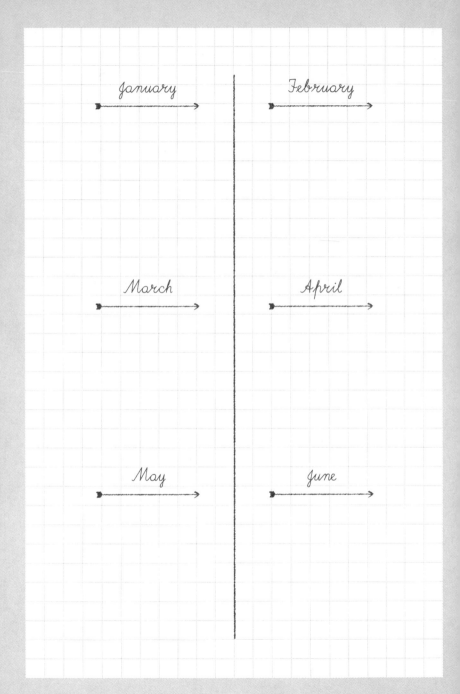

January

February

March

April

May

June

	jan	feb	mar	apr	may	jun
1						
2	O					
3						
4			O			
5	O					
6						
7						
8						
9						
10						
11						
12						
13						
14						
15						
16						
17						
18						
19						
20						
21						
22						
23						
24						
25						
26						
27						
28						
29						
30						
31						

MONTHLY

Now, your Monthly page. This is a great place to make a note of key appointments and dates so that you can look at the month ahead at a glance. Check your Future Log for any such instances. Don't be tempted to replicate this for the months ahead. You'll create a new Monthly page at the start of every month to stay as up-to-date as possible. Now index it.

1 T	
2 F	
3 S	Dinner with Olivia
4 S	
5 M	Sales presentation
6 T	Birthday
7 W	
8 T	
9 F	
10 S	
11 S	
12 M	
13 T	
14 W	
15 T	
16 F	
17 S	
18 S	
19 M	
20 T	
21 W	
22 T	
23 F	Weekend away
24 S	
25 S	
26 M	
27 T	
28 W	
29 T	
30 F	
31 S	

M	T	W	T	F	S	S
			1	2	3	4
5	6	7	8	9	10	11
12	13	14	15	16	17	18
19	20	21	22	23	24	25
26	27	28	29	30	31	

	all day	morning	evening
1 T			
2 F			
3 S			
4 S			
5 M			
6 T			
7 W			
8 T			
9 F			
10 S			
11 S			
12 M			
13 T			
14 W			
15 T			
16 F			
17 S			
18 S			
19 M			
20 T			
21 W			
22 T			
23 F			
24 S			
25 S			
26 M			
27 T			
28 W			
29 T			
30 F			
31 S			

all day   *morning*

	all day	morning
1 T		
2 F		
3 S		
4 S		
5 M		
6 T		
7 W		
8 T		
9 F		
10 S		
11 S		
12 M		
13 T		
14 W		
15 T		
16 F		
17 S		
18 S		
19 M		
20 T		
21 W		
22 T		
23 F		
24 S		
25 S		
26 M		
27 T		
28 W		
29 T		
30 F		
31 S		

evening

M T W T F S S
              1 2 3
4 5 6 7 8 9 10
11 12 13 14 15 16 17
18 19 20 21 22 23 24
25 26 27 28 29 30
31

M	T	W	T	F	S	S
			1	2	3	4
5	6	7	8	9	10	11
12	13	14	15	16	17	18
19	20	21	22	23	24	25
26	27	28	29	30	31	

— — — — — —

1 T	
2 F	
3 S	
4 S	
5 M	
6 T	
7 W	
8 T	
9 F	
10 S	
11 S	
12 M	
13 T	
14 W	
15 T	
16 F	
17 S	
18 S	
19 M	
20 T	
21 W	
22 T	
23 F	
24 S	
25 S	
26 M	
27 T	
28 W	
29 T	
30 F	
31 S	

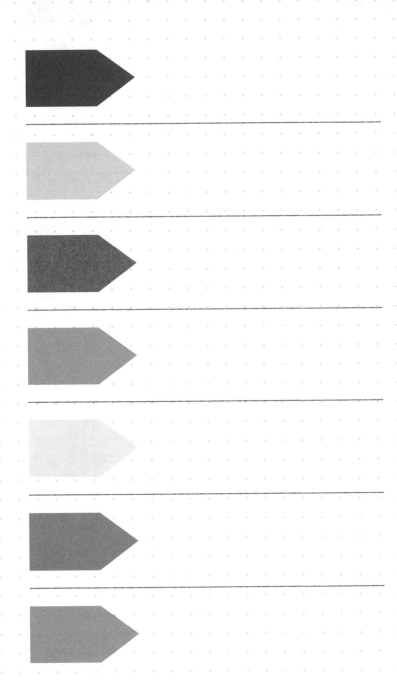

WEEKLY

As you'd guess, this page provides the opportunity to sit down and look at the week ahead. Make a habit of sitting down on Sunday evenings to write this page and noting down any appointments, social events or deadlines you have coming up. Even if your plans go haywire, this routine will provide a sense of ease and mindfulness.

M

T

W

T

F

S

S

notes

goals

10 Monday

_____
_____
_____
_____
_____
_____

Tuesday

_____
_____
_____
_____
_____
_____

11

12

Wednesday

_____
_____
_____
_____
_____
_____

M / 10	T / 11	W / 12	T / 13

tasks

projects

_____

_____

_____

_____

_____

_____

_____

F / 14	S / 15	S / 16

notes

.

personal

21

22

23

24

25

26
27

mon

tues

wed

thur

fri

sat

sun

— goals —

MONDAY

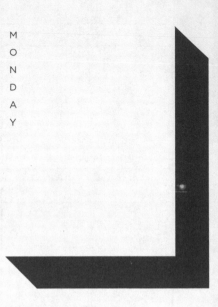

Today

DAILY

Hopefully you've kept the coded bullet list we created in the key (see pp. 13–14) at the start of your book going. Daily pages are, at their most basic, where you keep that list. Again, no need to add these ahead of time because your Weekly, Monthly and Future Log have you covered. You might not use a page a day, so if you only use a quarter page for a day's list, go ahead and start the next day on the same page. You don't need to index these, unless you want to.

Don't feel obliged to create a Yearly, Future Log, Monthly and Weekly if you don't want to—this is your journal so pick the combination that you know will keep you the most organized. If you're not sure, try them all out and eliminate as necessary.

16

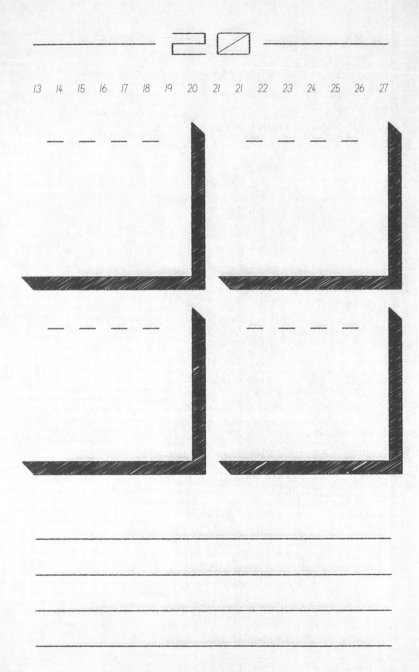

MONDAY

Monday

- [ ] _____
- [ ] _____
- [ ] _____
- [ ] _____
- [ ] _____

Tuesday

M	T	W	T	F	S	S
				1	2	3
4	5	6	7	8	9	10
11	12	13	14	15	16	17
18	19	20	21	22	23	24
25	26	27	28	29	30	31

Monday

_____

_____

_____

_____

_____

_____

_____

Today's inspiration

FRI

16

TRACKERS

A Tracker is a visual way of monitoring your goals. They tend to work best when set over a month but you can try a weekly period if you like. Set your days over one axis and the habits you're monitoring over the other. You can check off boxes or use color coding—experiment!

Variations

Some goals don't need to be completed every day. Use this calendar method to track recurring irregular goals.

	S	S	M	T	W	T	F	S
	1	2	3	4	5	6	7	8
Run three times a week								
Drink 2L of water	●		●			●	●	
No snacking between meals								
Speak up in meetings								
Tidy one area		✕				✕		✕
Reply to emails			♥				♥	
Read book			✓				✓	

T	W	T	F	S	S	M	T	W	T	F	S	S	M	T	W	T	F	S	S	M
11	12	13	14	15	16	17	18	19	20	21	22	23	24	25	26	27	28	29	30	31
●			●	●				●									●	●		
✕			✕	✕							✕	✕	✕		✕		✕	✕	✕	
						♥		♥												
	✓							✓						✓						

THREADING

Filled up a page and want to start another one? Keep track of multiple pages by adding the next page number of your spread in brackets to the right of the page number of the first page. Add the number of the previous page in brackets on the left-hand side in case you need to refer back.

52 (62) / (52) < 62

COLLECTIONS

Now you've got the basics down, it's time to start having some fun. Collections are an easy way to group themed lists together. They are particularly helpful for long-term tasks that you don't necessarily want to clog up your to-do lists. Reading lists, films to watch, home improvements, a work project . . . Don't forget to index them!

CHECKING IN

As you start to use your bullet book more often, you will organically realize which parts of the journal work for you and which don't. Perhaps you'll enjoy the forensic attention to detail that a bullet book can allow or maybe you'll find that you only use your book for to-do lists. Try not to add too many new spreads at one time or you might find yourself struggling to keep up.

Remember: everybody is different and whatever works for you is the best way. There is no point trying to struggle on with something that isn't right for you. You might want to take a moment at the end of each month to evaluate which aspects have worked for you and which haven't, and make a note of the new things you would like to try. You can then modify the way that you use your journal as each month progresses. The ultimate aim is to create a journal that works for you.

GET CREATIVE I

Spaced throughout this book are exercises and creative ideas
to help you to decorate and personalize your bullet book.
Don't worry if you can't imitate the clean, sharp lines shown
in this book; you'll find your own style.

BULLET VARIATIONS

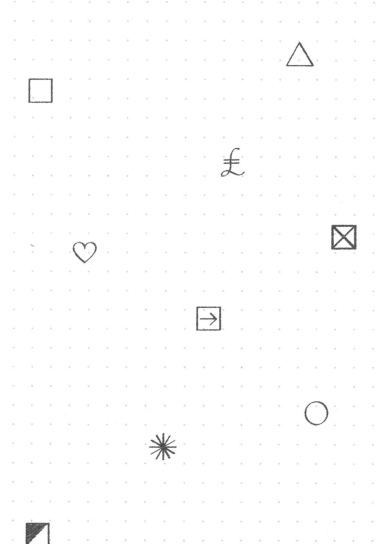

DOODLES

You don't have to be an artist or even remotely creative to add some decoration to your bullet book. Try copying these simple doodles to bring your pages to life.

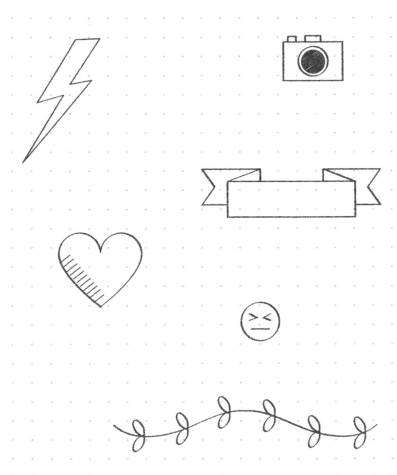

BLOCK LETTERING

Mastering a variety of lettering styles will help your headers stand out. Once you've got the hang of this blocked style, use the quotes dotted throughout the book to practice using it in full words and sentences.

ABCDEFGHIJ
KLMNOPQRS
TUVWXYZ

- -

abcdefghijk
lmnopqrstuv
wxyz

× × × × × × × × × × × × × × × × × × × ×

1234567890
!?()""

FIXING MISTAKES

As frustrating as ruining a spread may be, try not to get too caught up in making your journal look perfect. Practical use is more important than style. However, if you can't help but get a wave of irritation every time you spot that smudge, strike-through, or scribbled-out page, then correction fluid, masking tape, washi tape and origami paper can help turn a mistake into a flourish.

CREATIVITY

— IS —

CONTAGIOUS

PASS

IT ON

Albert Einstein

WORK SMARTER, NOT HARDER

Whether you work in an office, are self-employed, at school or job hunting, your bullet book can help you keep track of projects, organize your time and evaluate your progress. Here you'll also find tips to increase your productivity. Super efficiency, here we come!

USING MIGRATION TO
BECOME MORE EFFICIENT

Chronic procrastinator? One effective way of using your
bullet book for productivity is to give yourself a limit on
the number of times you can migrate any one task. Create
a Star Chart and allow yourself a reward for every tenth
task you complete within these limits. Respond better to a
crack of the whip? Try a Wall of Shame chart and sanction
yourself if you procrastinate. If self-discipline is not your
strong suit, ask a willing friend or colleague to check in on
your page once a week.

DO FIVE THINGS

Overwhelmed by your to-do list? Write down the five most important that you must do today. If you have difficulty prioritizing then pick out the tasks that will generate the most happiness or overall productivity or money for others on completion. Work through them in order, and turn your phone or email off to reduce distractions. Got through those five things? Turn your attention to one easy task and then go right back and make your next top five list.

TEN-BY-TEN

Have a list of tasks that you're forever procrastinating on? Try a ten-by-ten. Make a list of ten tasks and tackle one every day. Give yourself a reward if you manage to complete every task in ten days.

Tip: If there's one task, conversation or job you're dreading, tackle that one first.

TIME BAR

If you need to plan your day carefully, try adding a time bar to your Daily to allocate timeframes to your tasks and meetings. Remember to allow time for breaks. Alternatively, if you need to keep track of time spent on various projects then shade in your categories after the event.

THE 365 RULE

If a task will take less than 365 seconds, don't add it to your list, calendar or Future Log, just do it. If you like to keep a record, or find the act of crossing off soothing, then consider keeping tally rather than taking the time to write every small task out.

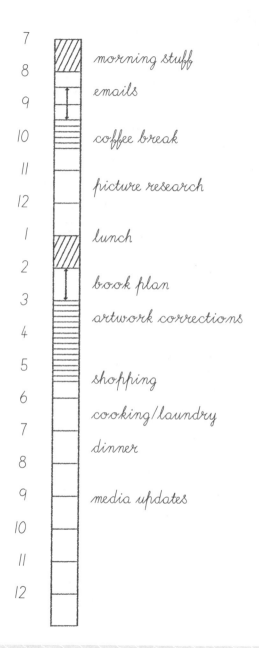

7
8   morning stuff
    emails
9
10 coffee break
11 picture research
12
1   lunch
2
    book plan
3   artwork corrections
4
5
    shopping
6   cooking/laundry
7   dinner
8
9   media updates
10
11
12

EXAM AND STUDY TIPS

Exams can be a stressful part of school and working life, and can often feel anxiety-inducing. Studying for them is the first step. As you prepare, take notes of what works and doesn't work for you, so that you can formulate your perfect set-up and refer back to your list the next time exam season comes around.

- Do you structure your time by the hour or do you prefer to shift focus as required?

- Do you prefer working with friends, in a library, at home or in a café?

- What are your favorite snacks and what foods make you lethargic?

- Which memory-aids work for you: index cards to test yourself with or sticky notes around your house, perhaps?

WRITER'S BLOCK

Starting a report, essay or any long-form piece of writing can be daunting. Dedicate a page to noting down some prompt questions and sample structures to help you get those words on the page. For example:

Context / Issue / Action / Goal / Results

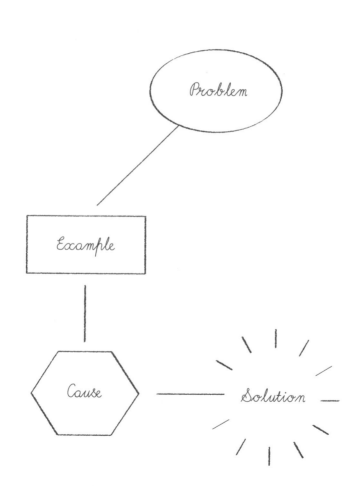

Problem

Example

Cause — Solution

STUDY SPRINTS

With phones, computers, tablets and the Internet at our fingertips, getting your brain into gear to complete some meaningful study can be tricky. So why not use your bullet book to help? Study sprints are half-hour periods of intensive work, whether that be note-taking or reading a textbook, where you get rid of your usual distractions.

Draw boxes to represent your sprints and write what you plan to cover in each. Turn off your phone and computer, and set a timer for half an hour. When your alarm goes off, if you feel like you achieved that "sprint" and kept away from distractions, then color the box in.

Remember, you may be tempted to study from the moment you get up until late into the evening, but it has been proven that taking breaks is vital for concentration and retaining large chunks of information. So take that coffee break with the peace of mind that, with efficient planning, you'll achieve what needs to be done.

Day	Subject	Subject
1	■ ■ □ □	□ □ □ □

DAILY SUBJECT STUDY PLANS

When you're studying for a number of exams it can often be hard to keep track of all the different subjects you need to cover. Create daily individual subject study plans to keep you focused and make sure that you don't leave anything out. You could set this up to look like a piece of old-fashioned lined note paper. Draw a margin down the left-hand side of the page and at the top put your subject title, e.g., Biology. List and number the topics you want to cover in one day. Be realistic about how much you think you can cover in a day—try four to five topics to begin with. For example:

Biology

1/ Photosynthesis
2/ Food chains
3/ The carbon cycle
4/ Environmental change

You can then cross modules off as you go along. Repeat the process for any other subjects you plan to tackle in that day, and highlight any that you need to come back to. If you're feeling more ambitious, you could set up your individual subject study plan for the week, separating out the topics by day.

BIOLOGY	M	T	W	T	F	S	S
Photosynthesis	●				○		
Food chains		●			○		
The carbon cycle			○		○		
Enviro change				○	○		

NEW SCHOOL YEAR, NEW YOU

When you get your new class schedule, there are a lot of things to remember: names, room numbers and class times. Create a table chart in your bullet book with the time frame on one axis and the days on the other.

	MONDAY	TUESDAY	
9		English	
10	Computer Programming		Comp
11	114		
12	Math	Math	Ma
1			
2	D 1		
3		Study Hall	
4			
5		L 3	

NESDAY	THURSDAY	FRIDAY
ogramming 1 1 4	_Computer Programming_ 1 1 4	
	Math	_Math_
	Computer Programming	_Study Hall_

WAITING FOR

Sometimes you need to wait for information or material from someone else before you can start a task. Avoid cluttering your to-do list with such items by creating a separate Waiting For list that you can add to your Weekly page or keep separately.

Waiting for:	From:	Requested:	Due:	Chased:
Digital brief	Jo	6/13	6/20	6/18 6/20

TO NOT DO

How many to-do lists have you written in your life? Hundreds, if not thousands? Take a moment to stop and think about the things you need *not* to do. Do you agree to projects when you're already overworked? Do you spend too much time in front of the TV? Mark your intention to better yourself by committing your bad habits to paper.

MAKE MEETINGS MATTER

If you regularly find yourself in never-ending seemingly pointless meetings, try to get in the habit of noting down what you need to find out, delegate or accomplish before every meeting. At the end of the meeting, check your notes, ask for any missing information and note your action points.

TRACKING DEADLINES

Use a monthly spreadsheet to keep track of multiple
deadlines and allocate your time more effectively. Go to
your next double spread and mark out the month. Divide
each day into sections and allocate each to subjects, projects
or classes. Note any key deadlines, meetings or exams and
draw a square around them.

F1 ● ▢	S2	S3	M4	T5 ✳
W6	T7	F8	S9	S10
M11	T12	W13 ▢	T14 ▢	F15 ▢
S16	S17	M18	T19	W20
T21	F22	S23	S24	M25
T26	W27	T28 ●	F29	S30
S31	● Project 1 ▢ Project 2 ✳ Project 3			

EVALUATING PROJECTS

Divide a page into four and use these classic prompts to evaluate any projects you're working on.

Strengths

Weaknesses

Opportunities

Threats

SPEAK UP

If you get nervous about speaking in class or in a meeting, you might find having a list of starter phrases on hand helpful:

- Just to play devil's advocate . . .
- I absolutely agree but I think it's important to clarify . . .
- I wonder if . . .

LEARNING A FOREIGN LANGUAGE

Learning a foreign language can be tricky, but why not try this tip: choose ten items from your home that you use every day and draw them in your bullet book, leaving a small space next to or under each one. Now, put sticky notes on the physical objects themselves. So your "wardrobe" becomes your *"garde-robe,"* or *"guardarropa,"* or *"kleiderschrank."*

At the end of the week, use a pencil to label your drawings without looking at the notes on the physical items. Did you get all ten? If so, draw up a page for another ten items.

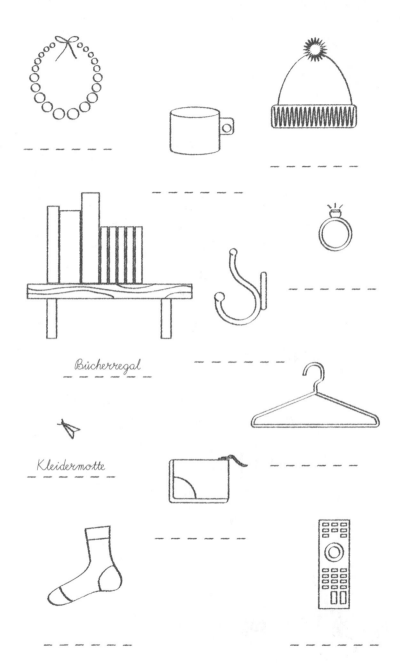

_ _ _ _ _

_ _ _ _ _

_ _ _ _ _

_ _ _ _ _

_ _ _ _ _

_ _ _ _ _

Bücherregal
_ _ _ _ _ _ _

_ _ _ _ _

Kleidermotte
_ _ _ _ _

_ _ _ _ _

_ _ _ _ _

_ _ _ _ _

_ _ _ _ _

THINGS I WANT TO LEARN

Keep track of your long-term goals on one beautifully illustrated page.

LEARN

TO DRIVE

Speak Italian

GUITAR

MILESTONES

Think of quantifiable targets you can reach at work and keep track of these. If you run a social media account, for example, you might want to track followers across different platforms:

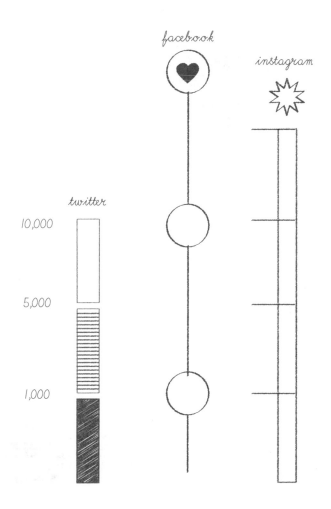

PROS & CONS

Facing a difficult decision? Keeping your method simple is often the best: try a pros/cons list.

WORK WINS

At the end of every working day, make a note of one achievement, however small. These records can be particularly helpful if you have a tendency to overlook your own accomplishments. Review these wins every month and create a collection of your key achievements to refer back to if you're in need of a confidence boost. These will come in handy when it comes to appraisals and job-hunting!

MONTH IN REVIEW

If you don't use your bullet book daily then a Month in Review provides opportunity for reflection.

- What went well this month and why?
- How can you sustain or repeat these achievements?
- What didn't go so well and why?
- How can you improve on these points?
- Did you achieve any quantifiable targets?

I dwell
in
possibility

Emily Dickinson

GET CREATIVE II

SOLVING SMUDGES

Inky pens can make your pages look beautifully professional but they have a tendency to smudge. Don't let your hard work go to waste by starting all over again—create a drawing out of the mark. Practice here:

BANNERS

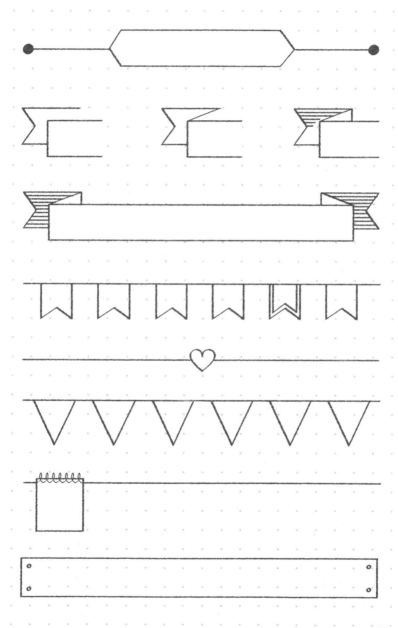

BOXES

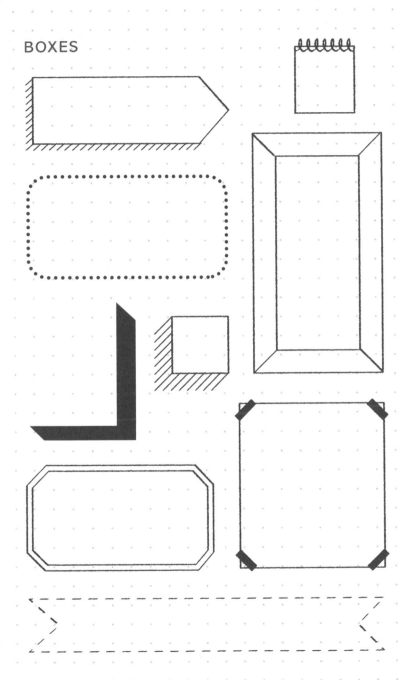

2019

HELLO

THANK YOU

NOTE

DOODLE—
HOW TO DRAW FLOWERS

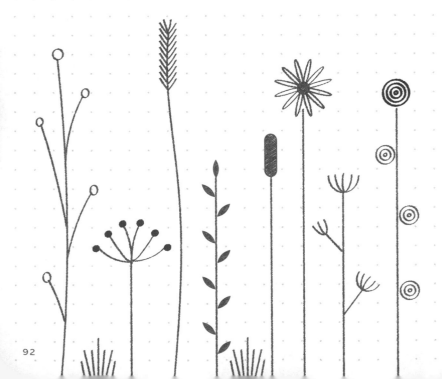

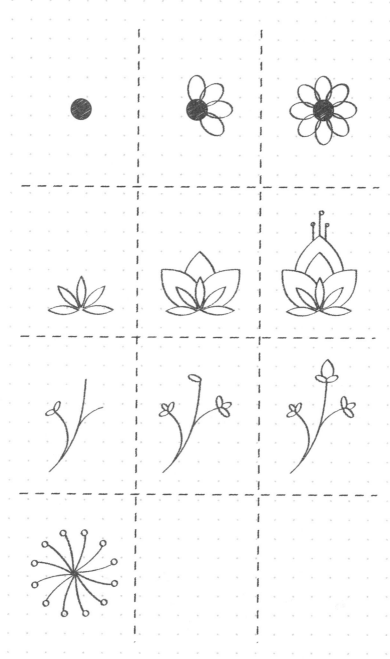

LUNAR CALENDAR

Lunar calendars are easily available online and can add
a decorative element to your Daily, Weekly or Monthly
spreads. Use these shapes to trace.

whatever satisfies the soul

IS

TRUTH

Walt Whitman

LOOK AFTER YOUR BODY

It feels like you can get an app for anything nowadays: tracking your sleep, mood, steps. They're all very well and good but finding the right one to fit all of your needs can feel overwhelming, and the focus on statistics can feel a little too clinical. Your bullet book can track your habits, help you toward achieving your goals and assist you to identify patterns in your well-being.

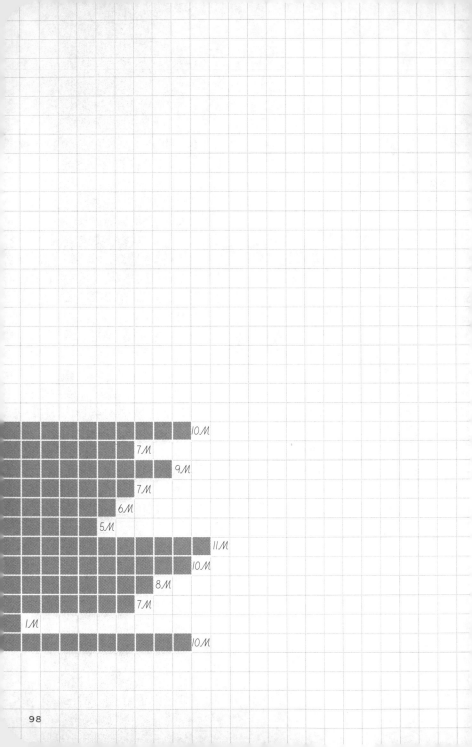

10M

7M

9M

7M

6M

5M

11M

10M

8M

7M

1M

10M

STEP TRACKER

How many times have you taken the elevator or an escalator
when you could have taken the stairs? Or jumped on a
bus when your destination is only one stop away? If you're
trying to be more active, start by walking more. Use a
pedometer or app to jot down your count at the end of your
Daily. Accompanying comments will help you to identify
patterns behind your step counts. Alternatively, set yourself
a target and create a mini calendar to keep track.

RUN!

Running through the countryside is great, but if you live in a busy city large green spaces can be hard to come by. Next time you're running, try to look up. What trees can you see? Create a simple box calendar and draw a tree for each day you run. When the month ends, you might have a thicket, a wood or a whole forest.

1–10 M

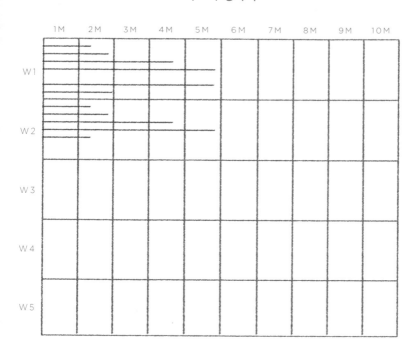

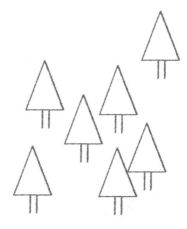

Variation

Get creative! What else could you turn into a tracker?

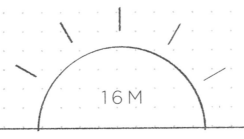

16 M

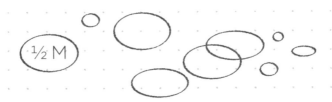

½ M

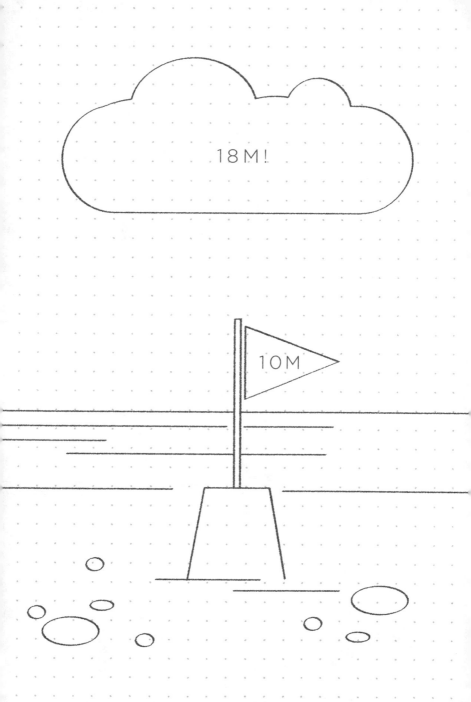

18 M!

10 M

WEEKLY MEAL PLAN

Put aside some time to plan the week ahead to ensure you never have to figure out what to cook in the evening.

INSPIRATION

Make a list of cookbooks you want, note your favorite go-to websites for recipes and the names of the dishes. Decorate your page and create collages from cut-outs or photocopies of recipes.

WATER TRACKER

Keep track of your water intake with this daily visualization.

Breakfast

1

2

3

4

5

6

7

Shopping

_____

_____

_____

_____

_____

_____

_____

_____

Dinner

Mon

Tues

Wed

Thurs

Fri

Sat

Sun

BODY WEIGHT TRACKER

Need to focus on losing or gaining some pounds? Color in each stepping stone as you go and reward yourself when you reach key markers.

Variation

If you keep a Weekly page and want to focus your mind on losing or gaining weight, add your weight or measurements at the start and end of each week in a separate box.

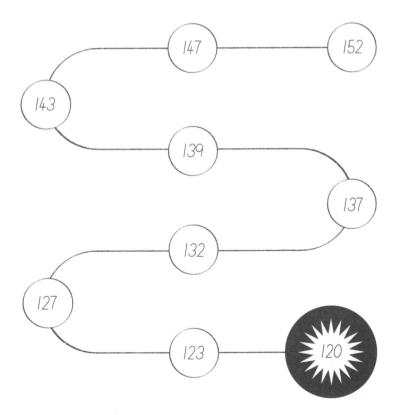

MONTHLY FITNESS TRACKER

If you want to see the amount of activity you do in a month then this page is for you. As this is a monthly tracker you should make it as visual as possible by using colored pens, adding stickers or getting artsy and portraying what you have done fitness-wise through images. Make it fun and easy to not only track but to review.

Tip: compare your monthly fitness trackers with one another: have you decreased, increased or maintained your level of activity?

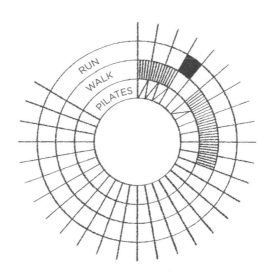

MEDICATION TRACKER

"Did I take my meds today?" Sometimes it's hard to remember, particularly if you need to take different pills at different times of day. Skipping or doubling up on medication can be dangerous. These trackers can also be useful if you care for another person, or pet! Cross out or mark your medicine as you take it.

M	T	W	T	F	S	S
● ○ ○						

MONTHLY SLEEP TRACKER

Monitor your sleep patterns with this simple tracker. Leave space to jot down any influencing factors.

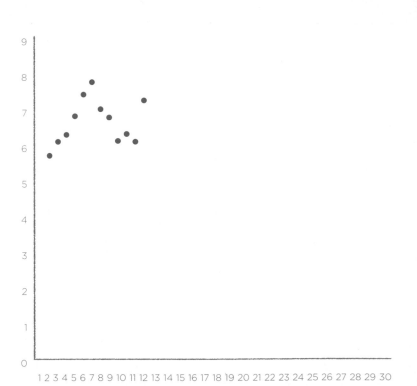

DATE	DRINK	UNITS	EFFECT
--/--/--		1 2 3 4 5 6 7 8 9 10 11 12 13 14 15 16 17 18 19 20	
--/--/--		1 2 3 4 5 6 7 8 9 10 11 12 13 14 15 16 17 18 19 20	
--/--/--		1 2 3 4 5 6 7 8 9 10 11 12 13 14 15 16 17 18 19 20	

ALCOHOL MONITOR

We all know that the quantity of alcohol you drink affects the severity of your hangover, but could the quality and type of drink you consume also make a difference? Does white wine give you an awful headache? Do whiskey shots upset your stomach? Or does beer make you feel fine? Use your bullet book to track your hangovers and see if changing your habits makes a difference.

- Draw a table and divide the top axis into four columns. Label each one as: Date, Drink (type of alcohol), Units, and Effect

- Once you have collated information over a number of entries, how about trying to change your habits to see if they make a difference to how you feel?

Note: Always drink responsibly and adhere to legal age-limits in your country!

FRUIT AND VEG TRACKER

Different countries have varying guidelines for how many portions of fruit and vegetables we should eat a day, with some suggesting as many as ten. Add your desired intake to a tracker or, if this is an important focus for you, use the one below, doodling a picture of the food consumed in each square.

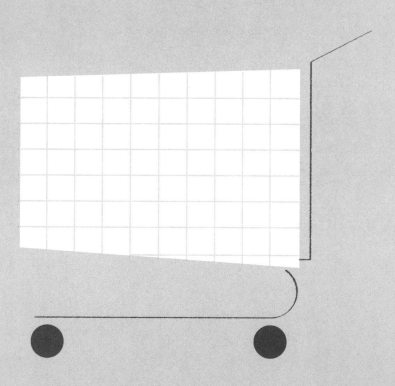

CAFFEINE TRACKER

Keep track of your caffeine intake with a simple tally chart next to your Daily or as a dedicated tracker.

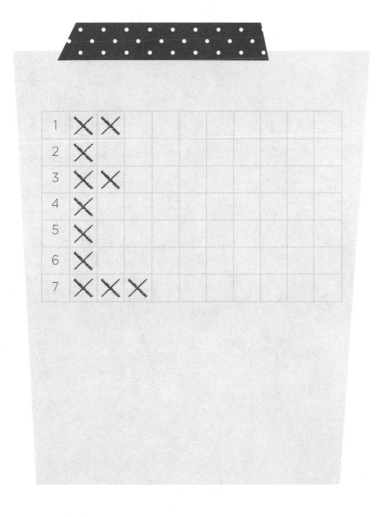

IT'S ALL CONNECTED

Want to see just how interconnected your sleep, mood and habits are? Track them all on one page to spot any recurring patterns.

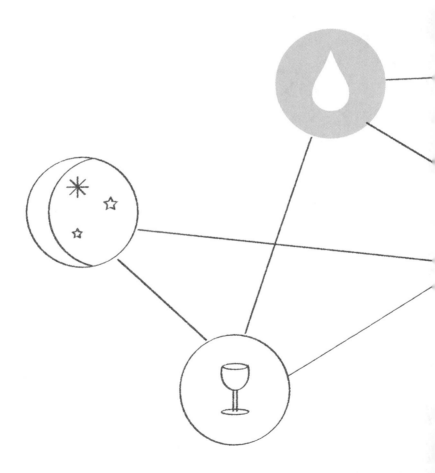

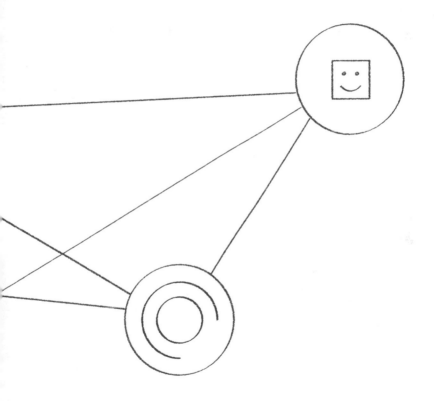

PERIOD TRACKER

Your bullet book is a great place to keep track of your periods and any side effects. A period tracker can be helpful if you want to plan around having your period on a special occasion such as a vacation, track your ovulation if you're trying to have a baby, or just to be more aware of your menstrual cycle.

You could either keep a note of your cycle in your monthly calendar or dedicate an entire page to track your periods over the year.

Draw a grid, with the twelve months along the horizontal axis and then thirty-one days down the vertical axis. You could leave space at the end of each month to note any patterns or concerns. You could include:

- The start and end date of your period, and length of cycle that month

- When you start/stop taking birth control (if relevant)

- The lightness/heaviness of your flow—perhaps use a symbol or color in the box to reflect this

- Moods/physical symptoms—e.g. aches, bloating, acne, nausea, cramps, bad moods

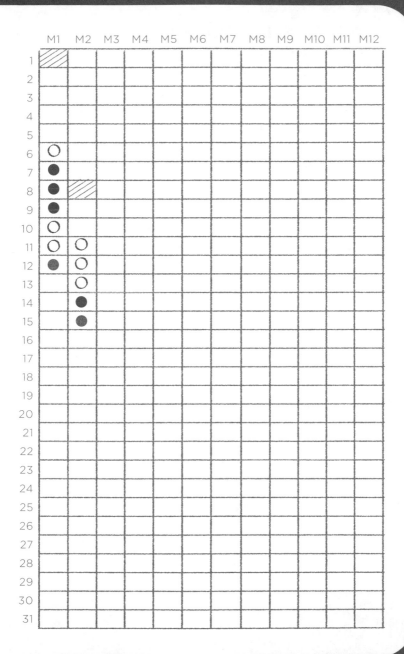

LOOKING AFTER YOUR BODY –
MONTH IN REVIEW

- What went well this month and why?
- How can you sustain or repeat these achievements?
- What didn't go so well and why?
- How can you improve on these points?
- Did you achieve any quantifiable targets?
- Targets for next month

GET CREATIVE III

USING COLOR

Experiment by using colored pencils, calligraphy pens, highlighters and gel pens to make your pages come to life. Matching a secondary color (for example, orange) with its analogous primary colors (in this example, yellow and red) will make the page feel harmonious. Complementary colors (yellow and purple, red and green, blue and orange) will make your page pop. Other color schemes could be focused specifically around pastel, metallic or fluorescent colors. Print a color wheel to stick in your book for inspiration.

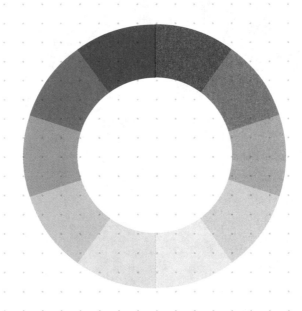

BULLET VARIATIONS

STRETCH YOUR LETTERS

If you want to write stylized titles but aren't sure where to start, practice stretching your own handwriting wide or trace these letters.

MORE BOXES

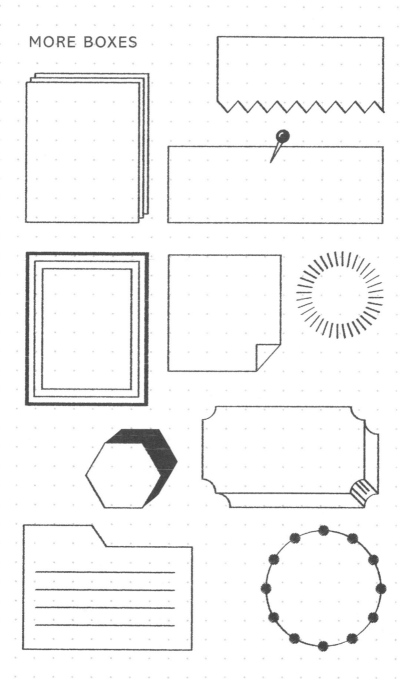

Keep
a little
fire burning:
however small,
however
hidden.

Cormac McCarthy

LOOK AFTER YOUR MIND

Your mental health is just as important as your physical health. For centuries, people have used diaries to record their thoughts and feelings. Your bullet book can act as a diary but it can also provide a more structured way of monitoring your mood, thoughts and feelings.

DIARY

USING YOUR BULLET BOOK AS A DIARY

If you choose to use your bullet book as a diary, you might want to keep your entries separate from your to-do lists in the book. Otherwise, intersperse them with the rest of your spreads, indexing them as need be. Lots of the spreads and activities in this chapter can be used as daily, weekly or ad-hoc journaling prompts.

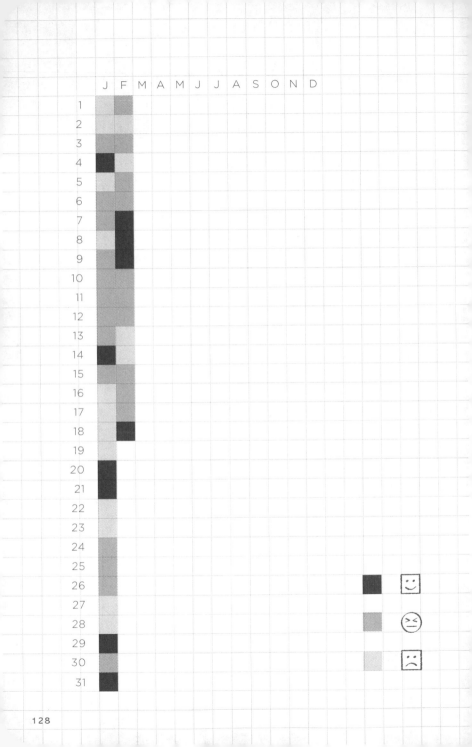

PIXELATED MOOD LOG

Keep track of the ebb and flow of your moods over the
course of an entire year with this pixelated mood tracker.

MOOD TRACKER

Keep a more nuanced record of your moods with this tracker.

	1	2	3	4	5	6	7	8	9	10	11	12	13	14	15	16	17	18
calm	■	■					■					■				■		
content		■	■	■	■	■	■	■	■			■			■			
tired				■	■	■			■	■			■					■
restless																		
irritated							■				■		■					
angry		■							■		■		■					
nervous																		
stressed				■					■				■					
depressed									■	■								
grateful		■				■												
adventurous																		
generous				■												■		

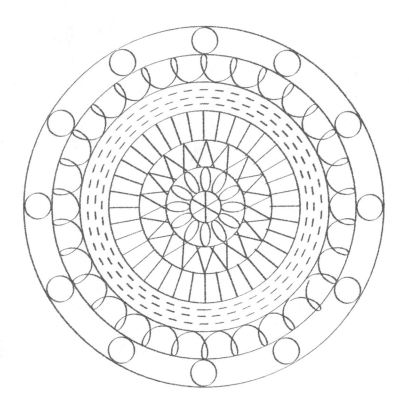

WEEKLY MOOD MANDALA

Create a mood mandala by drawing one large circle and then 6 smaller circles within so that you end up with a ring to represent each day of the week. Decorate each ring with a pattern or the day's name. Now pick your colors and allocate a mood to each. Color your mood each day and you'll end up with a beautiful representation of your week's moods!

Variations

- Split your circles in thirds to track how your mood changes between morning, afternoon and evening

- Challenge yourself to keep a monthly mood mandala

- Experiment with different shapes and patterns. Use the Get Creative sections in this book for inspiration

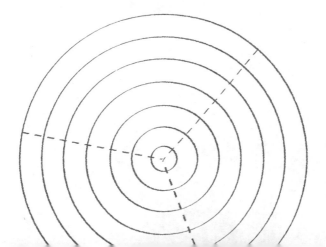

A–Z OF ME

Think of a word that describes you for every letter of the alphabet.

i	j	k	l	m
		K kind		
n	o	p	q	r

a	b	c	d
		C considerate	
e	f	g	h
n	o	p	q
	organized		
w	x	y	z

EVEN BETTER IF

Everything can't go perfectly all the time. Take moments
for self-reflection and note down what you might do better,
along with concrete actions you can take to improve
yourself. Try not to be too negative or hard on yourself and
think of these as positive, practical steps to becoming the
best version of you that you can be.

WHAT MAKES ME HAPPY?

If you've ever found yourself in a real funk, you'll know that
it can be hard to remember anything that makes you happy.
Keep a list here so you can remind yourself.

RAGE PAGE

Dedicate a page of your bullet book to vent your frustrations on when life gets a bit too much. Whether it's an annoying sibling, nosy neighbor, useless politician, horrible weather; nothing is too big or small. And as the old saying goes "better out than in."

This can be a monthly page or just every so often, depending on how much inner rage you have to express!

SET AN INTENTION

Focus your mind by setting an intention for your day, week or month. Spend some time making this intention stand out on the page with lettering, color or decoration.

POSITIVE PEOPLE

Make a list of the people who consistently make you feel the happiest, most creative, most beautiful. Those who make you laugh the most and fill you with joy and encouragement. Be sure to schedule regular time with these people—whether it's daily conversations, weekly calls or monthly dinner dates.

TODAY'S BEST THING

If you find it hard to think of singular things that you feel grateful for, ask yourself every evening: what was the best part of my day? Add this to your daily list or keep a separate page so that you can look back on your happy memories.

MONTHLY MEMORIES

Take time at the end of every month to look back on any important events, good or bad. If current affairs have had an impact on you this month, you might want to include these alongside your personal memories. Start by writing the month at the center of the page and then write each memory around it, perhaps with an accompanying picture.

GRATITUDE COLLECTION

Take time every day to recognize all that's wonderful in your life.

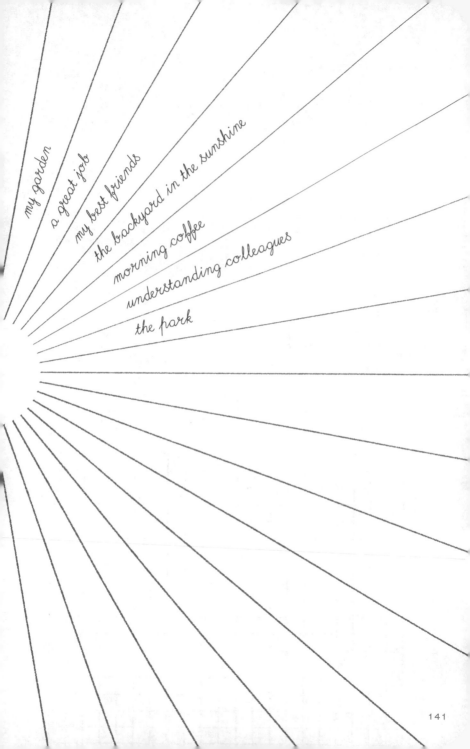

my garden

a great job

my best friends

the backyard in the sunshine

morning coffee

understanding colleagues

the park

RESOLUTION TRACKER

If there's one simple resolution you want to track over a year, use this tracker to check your progress at a glance.

JAN	FEB	MAR
♥ ♥ ♥ ♥ ♥ ♥		
♥ ♥ ♥ ♥ ♥		
♥		

APR	MAY	JUN

JUL	AUG	SEP

OCT	NOV	DEC

PAY IT FORWARD

Here's an easy way to make the world a better place. Keep track of every kindness another person shows you, whether that be letting you on the bus first, backing you up in class or in a meeting, or buying you lunch. Commit to repaying these acts of kindness to others in your daily life, and then some.

GIVE

The benefits kindness has on your body range from your emotional health, right down to your cardiovascular and nervous systems. In 1979, psychologists first coined the term "helpers' high," after a survey found that charity volunteers felt happier.

So if you're raising money for charity, keep track of it in your bullet book. You can monitor monthly, weekly or annual targets as well as practical tasks such as setting up a JustGiving page and listing who you're going to ask for sponsorship.

GOOD NEWS STORIES CHALLENGE

Let's face it: the news has begun to resemble a trash fire of late. If you're feeling despondent about the state of things, why not dedicate a page of your bullet book to focusing on some of the positive news stories happening around you, both locally and globally? No matter what happens there will still be people giving their seats up for old people on the train, cats rescued from trees, long-lost families reunited . . . Whatever makes you feel more upbeat about the state of the world, note it down in this section.

GOOD NEWS

Child mortality is down

Tiger numbers are growing

The ozone layer is repairing itself

Portugal ran its entire nation solely on renewable energy for four days straight

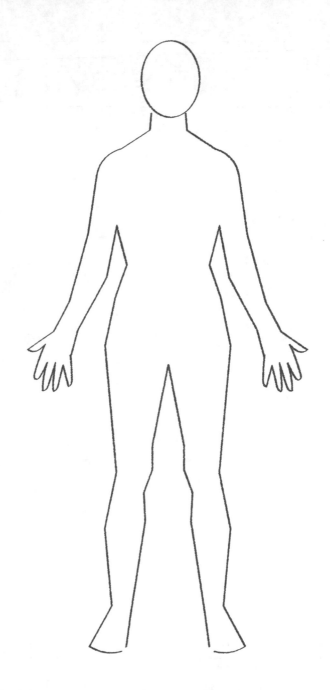

BODY SCAN

If you're feeling stressed or anxious, close your eyes and pay attention to each part of your body, noting (but not dwelling on) any tension, aches or pains. Keep track of these on a body chart. Tackle any recurring problems with a yoga exercise or self-massage.

WORRY DIARY

Reduce anxiety by putting your worries on paper and analyzing the situation. You'll soon find a solution, or realize you needn't be stressed at all.

Date	Situation	Worry	Anxiety
			1 3 2 4 5
Solution?			

WORRY FIXER

Is there a practical solution to your worry?

What are the solutions to this problem and the strengths/
weaknesses to these solutions?

Which solution are you going to implement and how?

How did it go?

___ ___ ___ ___ ___ ___ ___ ___ ___ ___

___ ___ ___ ___ ___ ___ ___ ___ ___ ___

___ ___ ___ ___ ___ ___ ___ ___ ___ ___

___ ___ ___ ___ ___ ___ ___ ___ ___ ___

___ ___ ___ ___ ___ ___ ___ ___ ___ ___

___ ___ ___ ___ ___ ___ ___ ___ ___ ___

___ ___ ___ ___ ___ ___ ___ ___ ___ ___

___ ___ ___ ___ ___ ___ ___ ___ ___ ___

___ ___ ___ ___ ___ ___ ___ ___ ___ ___

___ ___ ___ ___ ___ ___ ___ ___ ___ ___

___ ___ ___ ___ ___ ___ ___ ___ ___ ___

___ ___ ___ ___ ___ ___ ___ ___ ___ ___

___ ___ ___ ___ ___ ___ ___ ___ ___ ___

___ ___ ___ ___ ___ ___ ___ ___ ___ ___

SELF-CARE IDEAS

In our hectic world it is really easy to get sidetracked by work, the news and the needs of others, so it is vitally important that you also take care of yourself. Looking after number one is essential for both your physical and mental health, ensuring that you are strong enough to take on whatever the day/week/month/year holds.

Your bullet book is not only a great place to note down what makes you feel good but also a way for you to track your positive habits. What constitutes self-care will vary with each individual but here are just a few ideas to get you started.

Tip: Try not to beat yourself up if you sometimes aren't able to accomplish a task you set out to do. Self-care is all about taking positive action and shouldn't be another source of anxiety.

- Do something with your time that is purely focused on you—go to a gallery, have a swim in the pool, catch a film that you've wanted to see for ages
- Take five minutes to just be still and in the moment
- Change your bedsheets
- Notice five positive things about the world on your commute
- Mute, block or delete negative people from your social media
- Get out into nature—sit in the park or walk along the riverbank at lunchtime
- Do a mini declutter
- Fix something that's been annoying you—a broken lightbulb, a button on a coat
- Take a different route to work
- Open a window
- Compliment somebody
- Write down a compliment that you receive
- Do a body scan and stretch out any aches
- Take two minutes to just take note of your breathing
- Do a routine activity mindfully—brushing your teeth, tying your shoelaces
- Help a stranger

LOOKING AFTER YOUR MIND—
MONTH IN REVIEW

The way you look after your mind might change from one month to the next. Don't be afraid to try something different or give up something that just isn't working for you.

GET CREATIVE IV

It is never too late
to be what
you might have been

George Eliot

DOODLE-A-DAY CHALLENGE

Improve your drawing skills with one doodle a day.

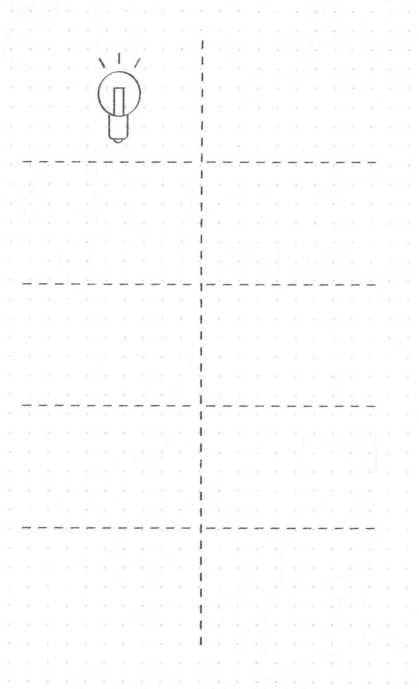

SQUEEZE YOUR LETTERS

Practice narrowing your handwriting or use these letters as a guide to create interesting headers.

ABCDEFGHIJKLM
NOPQRSTUVWXYZ

- -

abcdefghijklmno
pqrstuvwxyz

- -

1234567890

!?/" %()

TITLES

title

TITLE

Title

TITLE

TITLE

‹TITLE›

TITLE

DANCE FIRST

THINK LATER

IT'S THE NATURAL ORDER

Samuel Beckett

ORGANIZED FUN

Everyone loves a list! In this section you'll find plenty of ways to keep track of your hobbies and interests.

COLOR-IN MAP

Trace a map into your book and color the countries as
you visit them.

VACATION PLANNER

Money

Travel allowance _____

Accommodation _____

Food and drink _____

Activities _____

Shopping _____

Per day _____

Days = _____

Total _____

Currency bought ☐

Bank cards organized ☐

Bank informed ☐

Flights

Confirmed? ☐

Confirmation no. _____

Outward journey

Departure
airport _____

Terminal _____

Flight no. _____

Check-in time _____

Flight departs _____

Arrival airport _____

Terminal _____

Return journey

Departure
airport _____

Terminal _____

Flight no. _____

Check-in time _____

Flight departs _____

Arrival airport _____

Terminal _____

Accommodation

Confirmed ☐

Paid ☐

Address

_____

_____

_____

Contact tel. _____

PACKING CHECKLIST

- [ ] Passport
- [ ] Any required documents—visa, travel insurance, medical insurance card
- [ ] Currency and bank cards
- [ ] Shoes—sandals, sneakers, dress shoes
- [ ] Clothes—jacket, raincoat, shorts, trousers, tops, underwear, shirts
- [ ] Electronics—cell phone, tablet, laptop, camera, headphones, adapters and chargers
- [ ] Hairbrush
- [ ] Notebook/pen
- [ ] Toothbrush
- [ ] Toiletries—shampoo, conditioner, shower gel
- [ ] Mini first-aid kit—bandages, painkillers, antihistamines and stomach medicines
- [ ] Sunglasses, contact lenses/solution
- [ ] Sunblock
- [ ] Swimwear
- [ ] Make-up
- [ ] Books
- [ ] Razor

THINGS TO DO ON A SUNNY DAY

Hurrah, the sun is shining! To make sure you make the most of the good weather, why not use your book to note the things you would like to do when the weather is behaving itself?

- Sit in the park and watch the world go by
- Invite your friends over for a barbecue
- Get on your bike and explore a part of town that you have never been to before
- Find a quiet spot and read your book in the sunshine
- Eat ice cream!
- Organize a garage sale to make some extra cash
- Go for a swim in the sea or an outdoor pool
- Organize a picnic with your friends
- Find an outdoor yoga class

THINGS TO DO ON A RAINY DAY

You draw back the curtains, ready to start another day, and . . . it's raining. Fill your bullet book with ideas so that you're never stuck for something to do when the weather isn't behaving itself.

Indoor activities *(adults):*
- Knitting, sewing, crochet patterns you wanted to do
- Have all the ingredients ready for a relaxing bath
- Create some homemade beauty remedies
- Catch up on all of the films you've got queued up
- Start on your to-be-read pile
- Make some colorful cakes to offset the gray weather

Indoor activities *(children):*
- Finger painting
- Butterfly pictures
- Build a den
- Put on a play

Getting out of the house:
- Head to the cinema and wait out the bad weather
- Visit a museum or art gallery
- Go for a walk in the park and splash in the puddles
- Go to the spa and get your hair wet indoors instead!

THINGS TO DO ON A SNOWY DAY

It's freezing outside and all transportation has ground to a halt. Your bullet book is a great way to ensure you don't get cabin fever.

Indoor activities *(adults):*
- Watch a festive film
- Use this time to make presents or cards for upcoming occasions
- If a winter holiday is approaching, why not plan the meals that you'll be cooking to celebrate?
- Make a really indulgent hot chocolate
- Put together photo albums of your recent favorite pictures

Indoor activities *(children):*
- Make some iced cookies/cakes to reflect the weather outside!
- Have plenty of yarn, paper, and glue ready to make snowman cards
- Make some snowflake paper chains

Getting out of the house:
- Go and build a snowman
- Have a snowball fight with your neighbors
- Make snow angels

THINGS TO DO WHERE I LIVE

Got a free weekend? Not sure how to use it? Keep a list of ideas including new places to visit and favorite haunts. You can divide your list by categories (e.g., pub crawls, parks, museums, cafes).

BOOKS READ

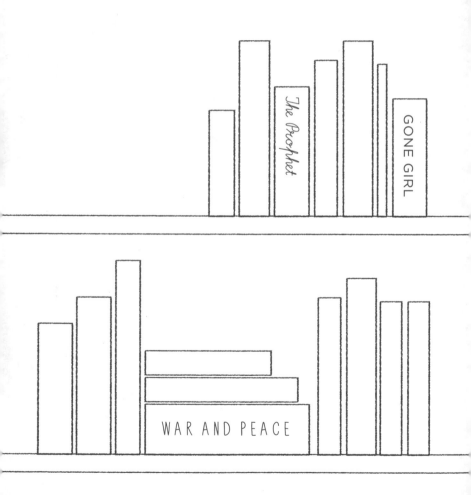

BOOKS READ: SCORING SYSTEM

Tracking how many books you read every year is a fun
exercise that allows you to see how your reading habits can
change over twelve months. Yet you may want to set up a
scoring system on a page separate from your Books Read list
that easily allows you to pick out your favorites (and avoid
the duds!) to pass on some fantastic book recommendations
to your friends.

- Split your page into two halves

- On the left-hand side, draw a series of lines in pen to
  the center of a page. Make sure each line is about half an
  inch apart from the other as you'll be writing book titles
  on each one.

- In the right-hand column, alongside each line you have
  just drawn, draw five small circles spaced out across that
  section of the page. Now, once you've written the title of
  the book you've read on the line, you can color in the
  dots dependent on your rating. 1 dot—"very poor, would
  not recommend," to 5 dots—"out of this world." If you
  DNF (did not finish) a book, leave the dots blank.

A Little Life
‒ ‒ ‒ ‒ ‒ ‒ ‒ ‒ ‒ ‒ ● ● ● ○ ○

‒ ‒ ‒ ‒ ‒ ‒ ‒ ‒ ‒ ‒ ○ ○ ○ ○ ○

‒ ‒ ‒ ‒ ‒ ‒ ‒ ‒ ‒ ‒ ○ ○ ○ ○ ○

BOOK EVALUATION

If you take your reading seriously then you might want to
dedicate a few pages to mini book reports with consistent
prompts.

RELEASED   STARTED / FINISHED

TITLE   FILM RELEASE

REVIEW   FAVORITE CHARACTERS

                            IMPORTANT STORYLINES

                            NOTABLE DEATHS

SERIES TRACKER

Obsessed with Harry Potter, The Hunger Games, Twilight, His Dark Materials, Millennium series, Game of Thrones or Sweet Valley High? Why not use your bullet book to keep a record of your reading progress and make sure that you don't miss the latest release?

RELEASED   STARTED / FINISHED

TITLE   FILM RELEASE

REVIEW   FAVORITE CHARACTERS

                            IMPORTANT STORYLINES

                            NOTABLE DEATHS

FILMS SEEN: SCORING SYSTEM

Whether your tastes verge toward brawny action films, silly Ben Stiller comedies or eye-opening documentaries, you can use the same system as your book tracker to rate your films so that when awards season comes around, you can decide what your film of the year is.

Start with a key to explain your rating system. 1 star for "truly terrible," 5 stars for "would happily watch again" or "would recommend."

You could include details of where you saw the film (that independent cinema with red velvet sofas? Half-asleep on Netflix?) and who you saw it with (a friend, an ex-partner, on your own?). You can also glue or staple your ticket stubs to this page.

FILMS TO WATCH

Keep track of the films you want to watch with this reel list.

Use a ruler to draw two vertical lines about 2 inches apart.
Draw a line a half-inch from the inside of each line.
Draw bold horizontal lines every 1½ inches down.
Add your film holes and you're ready to jot down your
Films to Watch list. You might want to add release dates to
films not yet out.

Add your rating as you work your way through the films.

Bee Movie
10/10

La La Land
6/10

The Handmaiden
00/00/00

BINGE-WATCHING TRACKER

If you tend to watch multiple TV shows at once, keep track of which episode you're on with a binge-watching tracker.

Variation

Love to rewatch your old favorites? Color code or add an extra dash for every instance watched. Mark your favorite episodes with a shape.

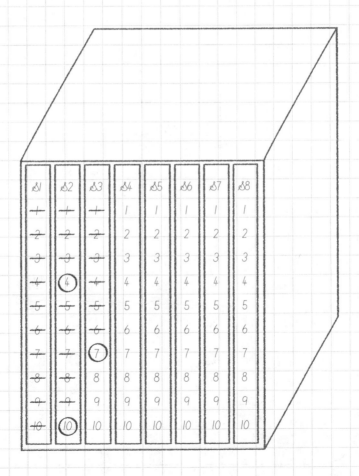

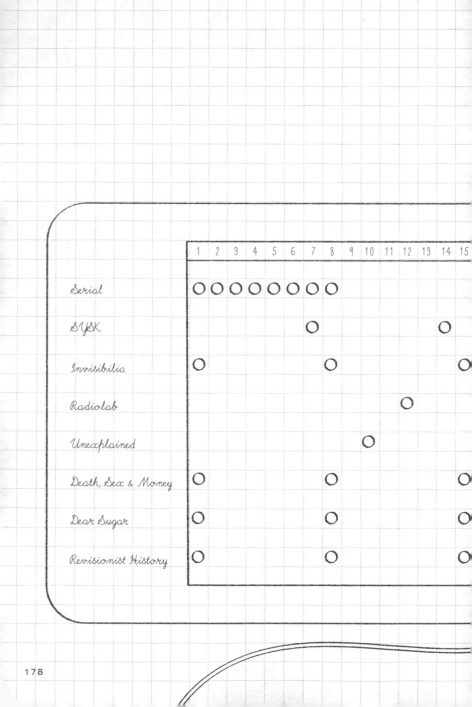

	1	2	3	4	5	6	7	8	9	10	11	12	13	14	15
Serial	O	O	O	O	O	O	O	O							
SYSK							O							O	
Invisibilia	O							O							O
Radiolab											O				
Unexplained									O						
Death, Sex & Money	O							O							O
Dear Sugar	O							O							O
Revisionist History	O							O							O

PODCAST PLANNER

Listening to so many podcasts that you can't keep track?
Plan ahead with this monthly grid:

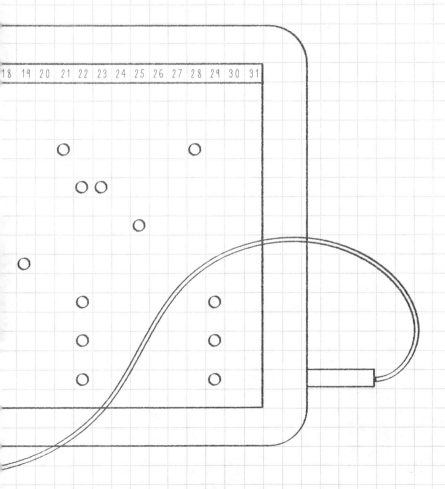

18 19 20 21 22 23 24 25 26 27 28 29 30 31

EVENT PLANNING

Your bullet book is the perfect organization tool for party planning. Dedicate a page each to the essentials, venue, guest list and budget. Here are some prompts to get you started.

Essentials

Catering
- Food and drink:
- Attendees:
- Budget per head:
- Selected caterer:
- Deadline for final confirmation:

Cake
- Preferred flavor:
- Personalized?
- Order deadline:
- Collection deadline:

Theme
- Dress code:
- Costumes?
- Color coding?
- Are decorations needed?

Timings
- Guests to arrive at:
- Entertainment required?
- Entertainment budget:
- Entertainment booking deadline:
- Speeches?

THE VENUE

First, decide what your requirements are. Once you've pinned these down and are ready to pick your venue, create a checklist to see which of your options best fits your criteria.

Capacity   Location

—   —   —   —   —   —   —   —   —   —

Outdoor space   ☐   —   —   —   —   —

Bar   ☐   —   —   —   —   —

Catering facilities ☐   —   —   —   —   —

Sound Equipment   ☐   —   —   —   —   —

Guest List
Draw four columns: one to list the names of your guests, and the others to mark when you've sent their Save the Dates, Invites, and whether they've RSVP'd.

BUDGET

Divide this page into 3 sections. The first column should have everything that you are going to need for the party, the next column should have an estimated cost and the last column should have space for the actual cost once confirmed.

At the bottom of the page, you should tally up the estimated cost and the actual costs and keep it updated. This will allow you to see very easily if you have gone over budget on one thing so you can see if you need to spend less on a different area of the party.

Items

Estimated Cost	Actual Cost

GAMES

Game enthusiasts, note the games you want to try and rate them!

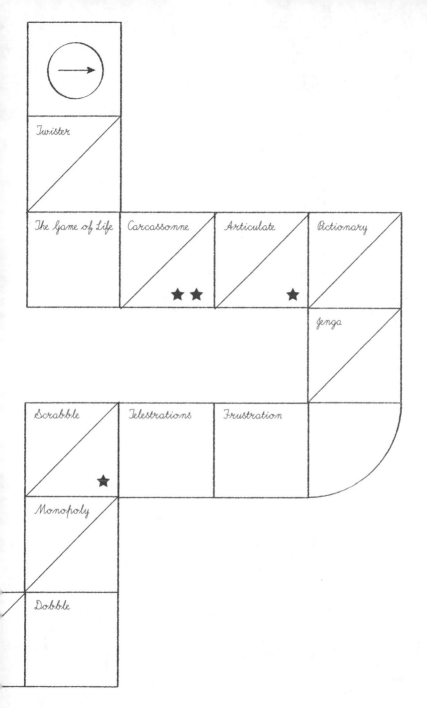

Twister

The Game of Life | Carcassonne | Articulate | Pictionary

Jenga

Scrabble | Telestrations | Frustration

Monopoly

Dobble

BUCKET LIST

What better place to store all the experiences and achievements you want to accomplish in your lifetime than in your bullet book? When creating your list, remember to take the pressure off yourself by writing your targets down in small groups, such as ten or fifteen things at a time, and include something you can do in the week you write the list to get the ball rolling.

Start by writing down the first thoughts and feelings that come into your head on a piece of scrap paper—this will then allow you to think about what kind of design you want to use in your journal to put the list together. These initial thoughts will be the most honest ideas of what you want to work toward as a future goal, so anything goes!

THE LONG-TERM BUCKET LIST

Create a bucket list, adding to it whenever you think of a new goal. Take a double page spread in your journal and in the middle, across the two pages, draw a circle (or square) making it as intricate as you like. Down the left hand side of the left page and the right hand side of the right page draw a line (straight or wiggly) spacing it out every half inch by drawing a square. These squares will act as boxes where you can add the number of your goal/target. Start on the left-hand page, number your box and write your aim. As you fill out more down the page, you'll have to write around your central circle (or square). You can bunch up or spread out your writing as much as you'd like by spacing your squares closer together or farther apart.

If you fill out your two-page spread, just start up another!

MONTHLY BUCKET LIST

Why not try a monthly bucket list for immediate goals like launching a website, or visiting your national art gallery? You'll probably just need one page for this, writing the month and "Monthly Bucket List Goals" at the top. You can make this page more minimalist than the long-term bucket list by focusing on using beautiful handwriting and quirky doodles.

1

2

3

4

5

6

7

8

9

10

FIVE-WORDS-A-WEEK CHALLENGE

Improve your vocabulary by picking five words from the dictionary at random. Make a note of your words and then write down a sentence using the word. Try to use each new word once a day.

THINGS I WANT TO MAKE

Life can be so hectic that our hobbies and passions can get left behind. Make a page of hobbies that you'd like to take up.

Baking

Jewelry making

Pottery

Knitting

Blogging

Writing

Pickling

Preserving

Origami

Foraging

CREATIVE-WRITING TRACKER

Whether you are a budding writer with a serious goal in mind or purely writing for fun and to boost your creativity, tracking your writing progress in a bullet book can be a great way to stay motivated in your writing journey. Your journal can be used to help set realistic goals and prevent writing burnout. It can help you to stay positive about your writing and what you have achieved so far, and stop procrastination and stalled progress.

- Set goals for a period of time in which you intend to write: write a number of words within a certain amount of time, or write consistently for an allotted period. Keep track of what you actually achieve.

- Keep a daily or weekly log of your writing activity. Use each log to reflect on your progress during that period of time: what days of the week or times of the day are you most productive?

- Keep a note of your mood after each writing session.

- Try to stay positive and focus on what you have achieved so far as a whole rather than dwelling on the negatives.

- If you are serious about writing a novel, you could devote a separate bullet book to help plan in further detail.

ASTRONOMICAL EVENTS CALENDAR

Keep track of astronomical events in your region with a specially themed calendar.

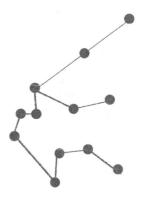

month						
M	T	W	T	F	S	S
				1	2	3
4	5	6	7	8	9	10
11	12	13	14	15	16	17
18	19	20	21	22	23	24
25	26	27	28	29	30	31

IDENTIFICATION PAGES

Avid bird-watcher? Botanist? Dog lover? Keep track of species you're on the lookout for with a dedicated spread. Keep spaces free to draw or note any species you can't identify yourself.

Manx Cat

- No tail
- Round face
- Elongated hind legs

American Goldfinch

Bluebell
(Hyacinthoides
non-scripta)

- White pollen
- Deep violet-blue flowers, occasionally white
- Flower stem droops or nods to one side
- Almost all flowers are on one side of the stem, hanging down to one side
- Flowers are a narrow, straight-sided bell with parallel sides
- Petal tips curl back
- Flowers have a strong, sweet scent

STATIONERY WISH LIST

Already possess the chief stationery items such as a pen, pencil, and stapler yet still want more . . . ? It can be hard to resist spending money on these useful (and often adorable) items. In this case, you should set yourself a budget and split your list into essentials and a wish list. Give yourself a waiting period before buying anything from your wish list to avoid expensive impulse purchases.

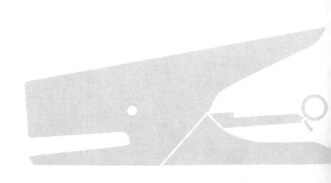

GET CREATIVE V

MORE DOODLES

DROP LETTERS

Experiment playing with the height of your letter shapes.

a b c d e f g h i j k l m
n o p q r s t u v w x y z

A B C D E F G H I J K L
M N O P Q R S T U V
W X Y Z ? & ($ £ € , !)

1 2 3 4 5 6 7 8 9 0

BORDERS AND DIVIDERS

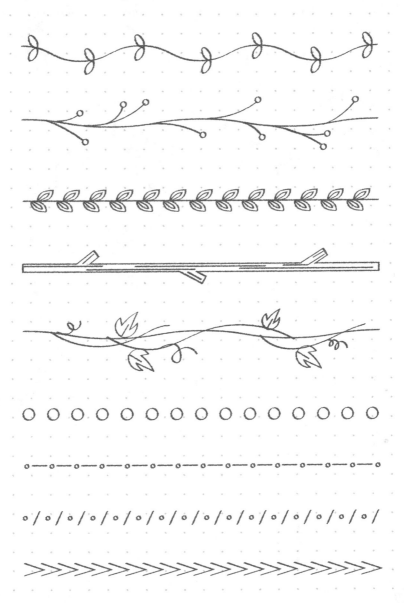

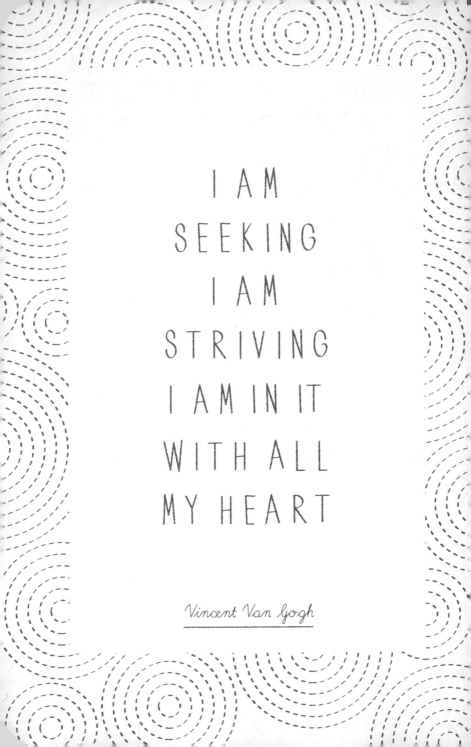

I AM
SEEKING
I AM
STRIVING
I AM IN IT
WITH ALL
MY HEART

Vincent Van Gogh

LIFE ADMIN

Do you always forget your aunt's birthday? Don't know what to have for dinner tonight? Did you forget to change your bedsheets again? This section will help you keep your personal and social lives in order.

BIRTHDAY WHEEL

Keep track of friends' and family's birthdays with a birthday wheel. Draw one large circle and then a smaller one within it. Now divide the circles into twelve segments and add labels for the month.

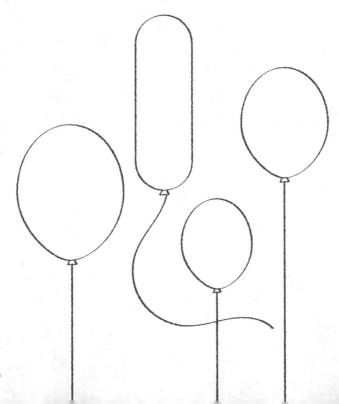

GIFTS TO GIVE

Ever see something you just know your best friend would love but then when their birthday rolls around, you can't for the life of you remember what it was? Never lose track again by dedicating a section of your bullet book to noting ideas for presents. Include shops or online links as necessary.

Decorations

_____

_____

_____

_____

_____

_____

_____

_____

_____

_____

Christmas movies

_____

_____

_____

_____

Guests

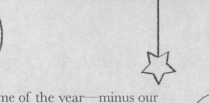

CHRISTMAS

It's the most wonderful time of the year—minus our birthdays—Christmas! Plan the best Christmas ever with dedicated lists of:

Gifts

_____

Recipient
_____

Gift
_____

Budget
_____

Amount spent
_____

Bought wrapped
_____

Purchase by
_____

Mail by

Christmas Dinner/Snacks

_____

_____

_____

_____

_____

Christmas Songs

_____

_____

_____

_____

COLOR-IN ADVENT CALENDAR

Divide your page into a 24-square grid and add your own
drawings or trace your festive favorites to count down
the days.

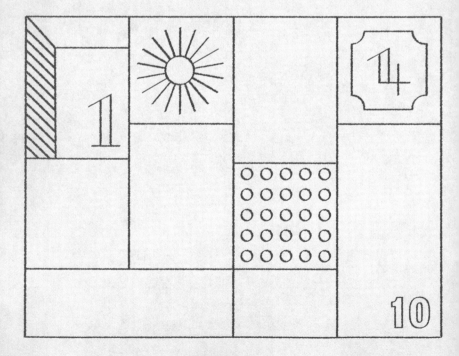

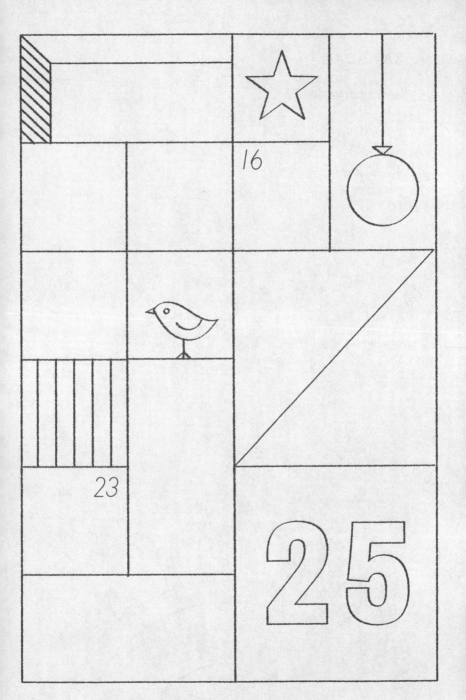

16

23

25

RAMADAN

Ramadan begins _____

Ramadan ends _____

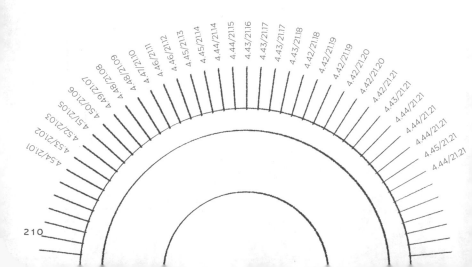

EID MUBARAK

As Ramadan comes to an end, celebrations for Eid, the
breaking of the fast, are underway. It's traditional to have a
sweet treat on the morning of Eid, so it's a perfect time to
try out a new recipe. Do a trial run first: would you make
any changes, or did it work well? Transcribe your version
of the recipe into your bullet journal. Use colors, images, or
fonts to make the instructions look beautiful.

Eid this year will be

— — — — — — — — — —

I will be celebrating with

— — — — — — — — — —

— — — — — — — — — —

on   — — — — — — — — —

at   — — — — — — — — —

We will eat

— — — — — — — — — —

— — — — — — — — — —

Eid Mubarak!

HANUKKAH

Hanukkah is a time for being with those you love. Draw a large circle in your bullet book and divide it into nine segments. In each, write the name of a friend or family member who you would like to catch up with over the next month. Use one of the handwriting exercises to practice your lettering. Whether it's dinner and a movie or a simple phone call, take the chance to talk. Don't forget to track the date in your calendar.

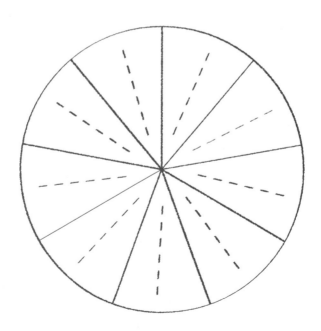

CHINESE NEW YEAR PLANNER

Chinese New Year this year will be

— — — — — — — — — —

It is the year of the

Rat	Ox	Tiger	Rabbit
Dragon	Snake	Horse	Goat
Monkey	Rooster	Dog	Pig

I will be celebrating with

— — — — — — — — — —

on — — — — — — — — —

at — — — — — — — — —

We will eat

— — — — — — — — — —

— — — — — — — — — —

I will give red envelopes to

— — — — — — — — — —

— — — — — — — — — —

Happy Chinese New Year!

FESTIVAL OF LIGHTS

Preparing for Diwali traditionally involves cleaning and decorating your living space, then filling it with light. Why not use this as a time to get some long-needed chores done? Take a page in your bullet book and draw a basic floor plan of your home. Title each room and label with the chores that need to be done. If you've got a lot of jobs and as many hands, write names by each task and delegate them. By coloring in each room as you complete the chores, you will light up the page!

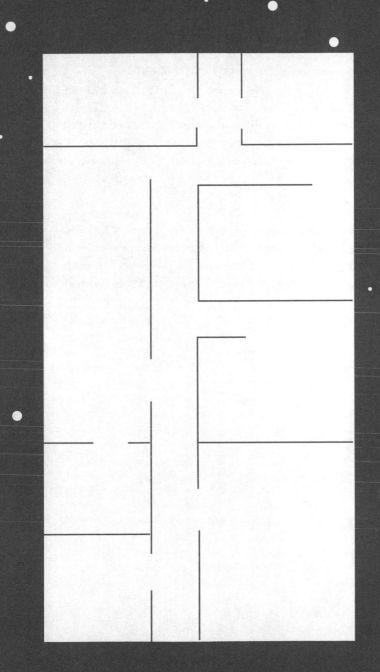

THE THINGS PEOPLE SAY

Dedicate a page to noting down funny quotes from people around you. It can be a hilarious thing that a stranger says on the bus, a teacher's bizarre catchphrase, a silly anecdote about a family member, or something that you and your friends can't stop giggling about. This page will be the perfect pick-me-up if you are in need of a chuckle, and a brilliant way to catalog memories of those around you so that you don't forget.

If there is a person in your life who is known for coming out with funny quotes, why not dedicate an entire page to them? Or why not allocate a page to a certain event so that you can remember all of the hilarious things that happened, e.g. on a trip with your friends, a bachelor/bachelorette party, a school trip.

YOU ARE ALWAYS ON MY MIND

In an age of social-media saturation and instant communication it can often be hard to remember to devote time to the people in your life who actually matter. Use your bullet book to set yourself regular, achievable targets to connect with your loved ones and let them know that you are thinking of them. Include these actions in your habit tracker if you want to be particularly self-disciplined.

- Phone an old friend you haven't spoken to in a while.

- Send a postcard to a relative from wherever you are in the world.

- Print off some photographs of you and your friends and send them for them to keep.

- Send flowers if somebody has a new job.

- Make a card and send a note to let somebody know that they are special to you.

- Or for those who don't want to use snail mail, send a longer catch-up email or Facebook message to somebody you haven't caught up with in a while to find out their news. It's much more personal than a "like!"

USEFUL CONTACT INFORMATION

While letter writing has become a thing of the past for
most people, there are still a few people that you'll need
to send a birthday card or thank-you note to. Rather than
keeping track of an address book, write down key contact
information in your bullet book.

NOTICE BOARD

Leave a space in your journal for your friends and family
to write messages to you to keep you motivated throughout
the day.

ONLINE DATING

Shakespeare wrote that "The course of true love never did run smooth" and although he was writing over 400 years ago, those who use online dating could argue that nothing has changed. Dating can be as exhausting as it is rewarding, so your bullet book is a good way to keep you focused on your goal, to ensure that you're spending your time chasing the good gals/guys and not expending energy on time-wasters.

- Collate ideas for your online profile: quotes that you wish to include, likes/dislikes, funny anecdotes, etc.

- Write down ideas for dates—restaurants/bars you would like to try, fun activities, favorite coffee shops.

- Track dates that you go on—keep a diary of the places you go, who with, and an "emotional log" to check in with how you feel after each date. Make sure you make time for breaks if you start to feel overwhelmed.

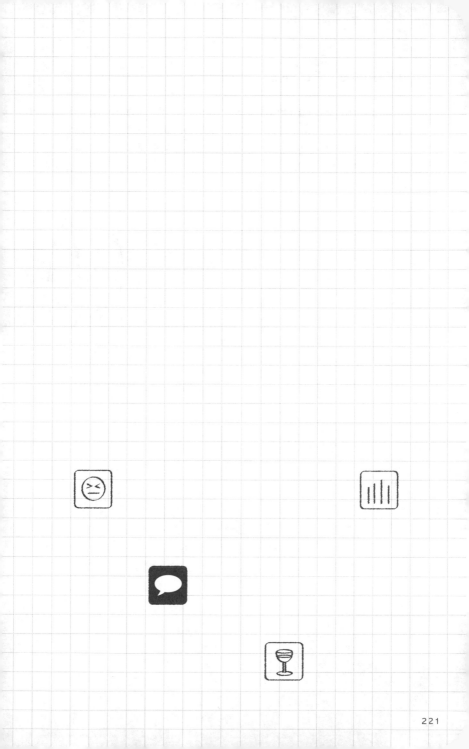

ONLINE ORDERS TRACKER

Online shopaholics know that it can be all too easy to lose track of multiple shipments. Make a note of the key information in your bullet book so that you never miss a returns deadline again!

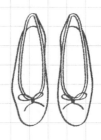

Date ordered

– – – – – – – – – –

Shop

Arrival time (est)

Returned

Refund amount

Refund due date

Notes

OUTFIT PLANNER

If you have an upcoming vacation, work trip abroad, or want to impress your colleagues in the first week of a new job, planning your outfits beforehand can take a lot of stress out of packing or getting ready in the morning.

- Draw a grid in your bullet book. On one axis add the amount of days that you need to plan for and divide the other axis into six or seven columns.

- If you need to plan a different outfit for day and night then divide each day column into two.

- Divide the other axis into the different components of the outfit: shoes, top, bottom, dress, outerwear, shoes, accessories, bags, etc.

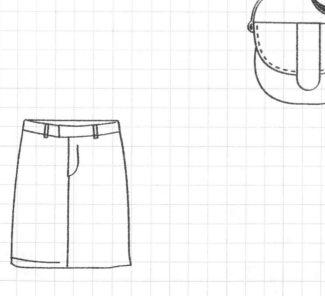

SAVINGS GOALS

Keep track of multiple savings goals with simple bars to color in as you deposit money. You can use correction fluid if you dip into your savings; hopefully the resulting uneven appearance will be enough to dissuade you!

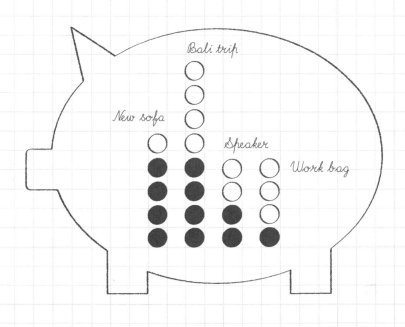

BANK BALANCE TRACKER

Make the first step to taking control of your finances by keeping track of your bank balance for the month with this line graph. Differentiate between multiple accounts by color. Alternatively, track the total amount spent each day.

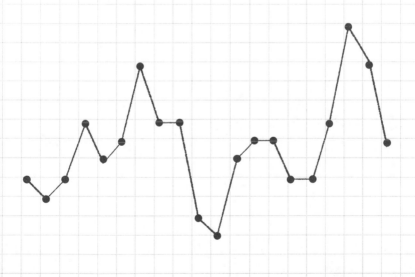

BEFORE YOU BUY

Impulse buying can eat into your everyday budget and stop you from achieving your savings goals. You might already be using your bullet book as a financial tracker: it is great for budgeting, working toward savings goals, and really analyzing where you are spending your money. Shopping can often have a huge emotional aspect so being mindful of this can be hugely beneficial. Why not use your bullet book to note down your feelings around money and to explore the reasons that prompt you to spend (good as well as bad)? Find five good reasons to buy something before you commit to it.

SPENDING LOG

Keep note of your transactions to be sure you know exactly
where your money is.

Start balance _ _ _ _ _ _ _ _ _

End balance _ _ _ _ _ _ _ _ _

Date	Shop	Item	Amount	Credit/Debit

RESTAURANTS TO TRY

We all love eating out whether it's frequently or a once-in-a-while treat, but with so many options how do you narrow down where to try!?

If you have ever forgotten a great review you've read, a recommendation from a friend or the mental note of a place that looked great—well, no more! It's time to take note! Let's start with headlining what type of meal you are after and jotting down the name of the restaurant or cafe that's come to your attention, then include details such as where it's located, if you can make a reservation and roughly how expensive it is.

If you're budgeting you may need to plan when and where you eat out. As your list increases each month you should summarize what restaurants you really want to try in that particular month.

→ LOCATION		♥ WANT TO TRY
$ BUDGET		✗ AVOID
O NO RESERVATION		
● RESERVATION		

BREAKFAST BRUNCH	LUNCH	DINNER
The Breakfast Club → East 17th $ $ O	Pizza Union → King's Cross $ $ O	sketch ♥ → Mayfair $ $ $ $ ●
Friends of Ours → Shoreditch $		Honest Burger → All over $ O
La Moka → Battersea $ $ O		
Sunday ♥ → Islington $ O		

AVOID

Yosma ✗
Marylebone
Average, overpriced

Chocolate
lava cake

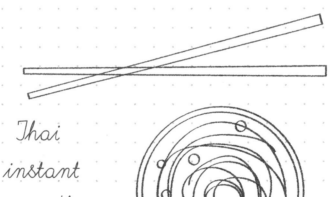

Thai
instant
noodle
soup

ULTIMATE COMFORT FOOD

Sometimes you need a hug in a mug! Research foods that can be cooked from scratch and cooked in a large mug. Draw a series of mugs on a page, decorate each one differently, and write the ingredients around the outside of the image.

Get creative! You could create a series of mug cakes or, if you're a savory person, a twist on instant noodles. Here are two recipes to get you started:

Chocolate Lava Cake
- 1 heaped tablespoon of melted butter
- 1 heaped tablespoon of caster sugar
- 1 egg
- 2 heaped tablespoons of plain flour
- 1 teaspoon baking powder
- 1 tablespoon of chocolate spread

Combine the first five ingredients in a large mug until smooth. Make a well in the middle of the batter and add the chocolate spread. Microwave on full for 90 seconds. Serve immediately.

Thai Instant Noodle Soup
- 1 serving of glass noodles
- 1 level teaspoon thai curry paste
- ½ spring onion, chopped
- 1 handful of beansprouts
- 1 handful of shredded spinach

Combine all ingredients in a mug, noodles first. Pour in enough boiling water to cover the noodles, then cover the mug with plastic wrap. Leave for 3 minutes and then dig in.

WEEKDAY DINNER IDEAS

Keeping ideas for dinner fresh and interesting every week can be difficult and sitting down to write your shopping list can feel daunting when you're busy, stressed or on a budget, particularly when all that foodie inspiration suddenly goes out the window. Storing all your favorite dinner ideas in your bullet book will help relieve that pressure while making sure you have lots of variety throughout your week. Planning ahead will also help to make healthy eating habits a priority as well as contributing to cost-cutting and better budgeting.

Variations

- Color-coding meat- and vegetarian-based dishes will help you keep track of your meat and veg intake for the week

- Group different cuisines together along one branch. Alternatively, you could group meals by how healthy they are, favorite to least favorite, or organized around a main ingredient, e.g., pasta, potato, etc.

- Make a note of preparation time beside dishes to help with decision making. If you know you have some busy evenings ahead, you'll know what dishes to avoid!

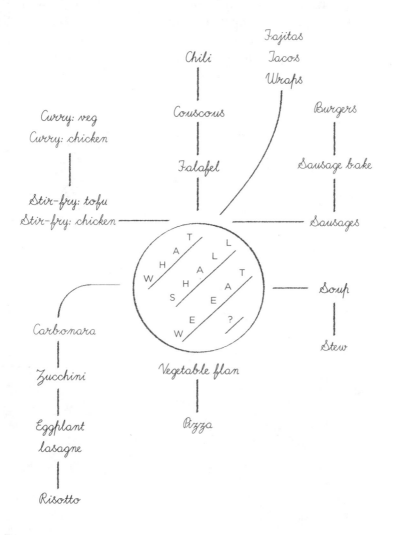

Fajitas
Tacos
Wraps

Chili

Curry: veg
Curry: chicken

Couscous

Burgers

Falafel

Sausage bake

Stir-fry: tofu
Stir-fry: chicken

Sausages

WHAT THE HELLS WEAT?

Soup

Carbonara

Stew

Zucchini

Vegetable flan

Eggplant
lasagne

Pizza

Risotto

POTATO PAGE

Which 'tater makes the fluffiest mash? Which should you choose for the perfect baked potato? Which spud makes great chips? Create a Venn diagram to make the most of this cupboard staple and you'll never go hungry again.

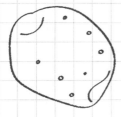

Russett –
Dark red skin.
For roasting, baking,
chipping, boiling.

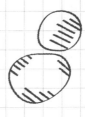

Red –
Pink skin, white flesh.
Chipping, steaming,
baking.

White –
White skin and creamy
white flesh. Boiling or
steaming. Delicious!

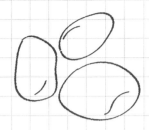

Yellow –
White to yellow skin,
white flesh. Baking,
mashing, roasting,
frying.

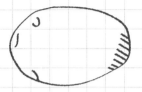

Yukon Gold –
Russet skin and light
yellow flesh with the
ability to be stored for
long periods. Baking,
mashing, roasting,
frying.

Fingerling –
Golden skin and creamy
white flesh. Chipping,
roasting.

MASTER CHORE LIST

BATHROOMS

- [ ] Empty and wipe down all cabinets and drawers
- [ ] Wipe down mirrors
- [ ] Wipe down and sanitize counters and sinks
- [ ] Clean bath and drain, tiles, taps and shower heads, toilet
- [ ] Wipe down doors, knobs, switches, skirting boards, etc.
- [ ] Sweep and mop floors
- [ ] Clean windows and window sills
- [ ] Take out garbage

KITCHEN

- [ ] Empty drawers and cabinets, wipe down interiors
- [ ] Wipe down cupboard doors
- [ ] Declutter and reorganize food cupboards and fridge/freezer
- [ ] Deep-clean inside oven
- [ ] Scrub stovetop
- [ ] Clean inside microwave and other appliances
- [ ] Vacuum under and behind fridge
- [ ] Change water filter in fridge if necessary
- [ ] Clean counters
- [ ] Clean backsplash
- [ ] Clean out dishwasher
- [ ] Wipe down and polish sink
- [ ] Sharpen knives
- [ ] Polish silver
- [ ] Wipe down doors, knobs, switches, skirting boards, etc.
- [ ] Sweep and mop floors
- [ ] Take out garbage

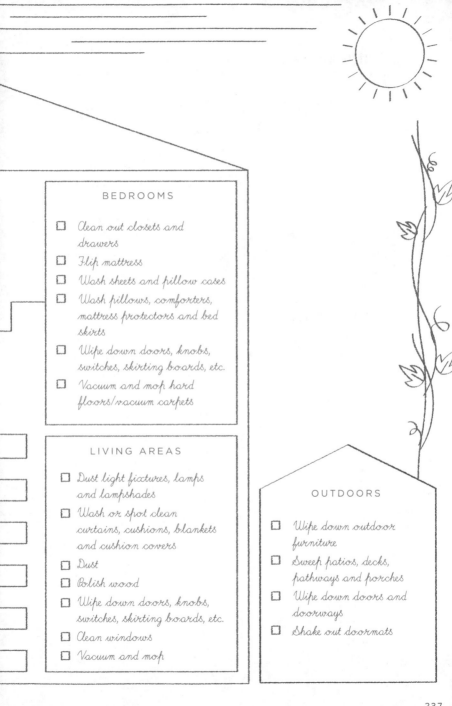

BEDROOMS

- ☐ Clean out closets and drawers
- ☐ Flip mattress
- ☐ Wash sheets and pillow cases
- ☐ Wash pillows, comforters, mattress protectors and bed skirts
- ☐ Wipe down doors, knobs, switches, skirting boards, etc.
- ☐ Vacuum and mop hard floors/vacuum carpets

LIVING AREAS

- ☐ Dust light fixtures, lamps and lampshades
- ☐ Wash or spot clean curtains, cushions, blankets and cushion covers
- ☐ Dust
- ☐ Polish wood
- ☐ Wipe down doors, knobs, switches, skirting boards, etc.
- ☐ Clean windows
- ☐ Vacuum and mop

OUTDOORS

- ☐ Wipe down outdoor furniture
- ☐ Sweep patios, decks, pathways and porches
- ☐ Wipe down doors and doorways
- ☐ Shake out doormats

SPRING CLEANING—
15 IN 15

With winter finally over, more sunshine and longer days,
it's time to kick-start spring! A great way of tackling a spring
cleaning, if you find the idea daunting, is to make it into a
challenge. Focus on one small area at a time, and tick that
thing off your to-do list for the day. Breaking the task up into
15-minute daily sessions makes giving your space a thorough
cleaning manageable—and means you're not faced with a
marathon session that will leave you slumped on the sofa
for the rest of the month. 15 minutes for 15 days and you're
done!

ANNUAL CHORES

Another way to keep track of yearly chores is to allocate
them to a month either in your Future Log or on a page of
their own.

jan Clean medicine cabinets and throw away expired medicines	**feb** Clean all the hard-to-reach places – behind the stove, refrigerator, washer/dryer, sofas	**mar** Steam-clean / shampoo carpets or polish hard floors
apr Wash windows (inside and out)	**may** Organize personal and household filing	**jun** Wash comforters, blankets and pillows
jul Clean and organize the garage and/or basement	**aug** Clean out drawers and closets. Donate usable clothing and items to charity	**sept** Wash walls and touch up paint where necessary
oct Defrost and clean freezer, stovetops, oven	**nov** Polish silver, wash china, dust inside the china cabinet	**dec** Organize kitchen cabinets and throw away expired items

WHEN DID I LAST . . .

Keeping on top of daily chores is one thing, but it can be tricky to keep track of the last time you changed your toothbrush or checked your smoke alarm. Your bullet book can help you to keep track of those pesky tasks. Start by making a list of all those chores/tasks that you tend to forget about.

Tip: You can also note down tasks in your Future Log so that you pick them up in your Monthly, Weekly and/or Daily spreads further down the line.

Task	Frequency	
Change toothbrush	Monthly	12 June
Wash bedding	6 months	
Clean fridge	2 months	
Check smoke alarms	6 months	
Flip mattress	3 months	
Defrost freezer	Yearly	
Clean car	3 months	

- Separate your page into six columns. In the first, list the tasks you want to keep track of. You may also want to make a note of how often you want to complete the chore, e.g. flipping a mattress every three months.

- Use the remaining columns to make a note of the date you last completed the chore/task. Every time you complete a task, make a note of the date.

- If you want to make your list look more quirky, instead of creating a simple grid, you could draw rectangles or circles all around the page for each chore/task, leaving enough room within each shape to keep track of at least five dates in each.

24 July

HOME PROJECTS—BY ROOM

Keep track of your home improvements wishlist with this visual aid.

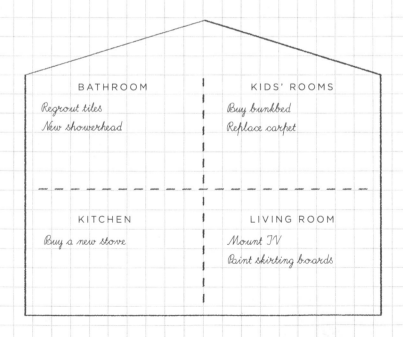

BATHROOM

Regrout tiles
New showerhead

KIDS' ROOMS

Buy bunkbed
Replace carpet

KITCHEN

Buy a new stove

LIVING ROOM

Mount TV
Paint skirting boards

MASTER GROCERY LIST

To supplement your weekly shopping lists you should also have a cupboard full of the staples that can last for weeks, or even months. What this will consist of will vary depending on your personal tastes, but it can be helpful to keep track of what you have and what you actually use regularly—before you end up with four identical packets of paprika. Below are some staple ingredients that should cover most bases. Keep a note of these in you journal for easy reference.

The essentials:
- Salt
- Pepper
- Garlic
- Olive oil

Dried herbs & spices:
- Dried chili flakes
- Paprika
- Bay leaves
- Cumin
- Turmeric
- Ground cinnamon
- Ground ginger
- Thyme
- Rosemary

Condiments:
- Soy sauce
- White wine vinegar
- Balsamic vinegar
- Vegetable oil

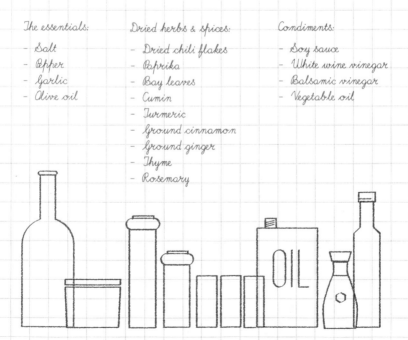

SOMETIMES THE DREAMS

THAT COME TRUE

ARE THE DREAMS

YOU NEVER EVEN

KNEW YOU HAD

Alice Sebold

GET CREATIVE VI

WEATHER ICONS

STEP-BY-STEP FLOURISHES

MASTERCLASS

CALLIGRAPHY

Use a brush pen or nib and ink to achieve the beautiful
varying lines of calligraphic writing. The key is to make
broader marks on your downward strokes and narrower
marks for your upward strokes. Practice at the back of your
book or on lined paper following the alphabet overleaf and
then using the inspirational quotes throughout the book.

A B C D E F G

H I J K L M

N O P Q R S

T U V W X

Y Z

a b c d e f g h i

j k l m n o p q

r s t u v w x

y z

( ) ! , " ? &

1 2 3 4 5 6 7 8 9 0

SECRET SPACE

If you find that for some spreads, a double page just isn't
enough, the next time you draw up one, go to a double
page. Cut the page on the left, leaving just a small square of
paper still attached to the spine. Repeat this process on the
next page. Voila! A spread within a spread.

RIBBON

Add multiple ribbons to your bullet book to ensure you can find your most frequently used spreads in an instant. Use strong glue to stick ribbons to the top of your book's spine. Knot the end of your ribbon to prevent excess fraying.

ADVANCED JOURNALING SHOPPING LIST

- Washi tapes
- Origami paper
- Wrapping paper scraps
- Rubber stamps and colored ink pads
- Brush pens
- Calligraphy pen, nibs and inks
- Watercolor pencils
- Water brush pen
- Glitter glue

USING SEPARATE JOURNALS FOR DIFFERENT THINGS

Are you a forgetful type? Never be without your journal: keep one at home for personal use and one at work or school.

Variation

If you're big on daily and weekly planning you might want to keep these pages separate from your collections and trackers by putting them in opposite ends of the book.

MIGRATING TO A NEW NOTEBOOK

A new bullet book is a chance to start afresh. Before you dive headfirst into your new book, take a moment to flip through your completed one. Consider what worked and what didn't. Which spreads will you continue to use in your new book and which will you leave behind? The same applies when migrating your to-do lists. Are there items on that list that have been postponed dozens of times? Do they really still need completing or can you let them go?

Remember, the possibilities are as infinite as your imagination.

ACKNOWLEDGMENTS

Text and project management by Zennor Compton with a huge thank you to rest of the *365 Bullet Guide* Dream Team at Macmillan for their stellar contributions: Saba Ahmed, Natalie McCourt, Joanna Dawkins, Bríd Enright, Sarah Harvey, Rebecca Kellaway, Rory O'Brien, Sarah Patel, Rachael Wing, Charlotte Wright and Alex Young, and Marcia Mihotich for the design and illustrations.